THE
CAMPAIGN
OF 1812
IN RUSSIA

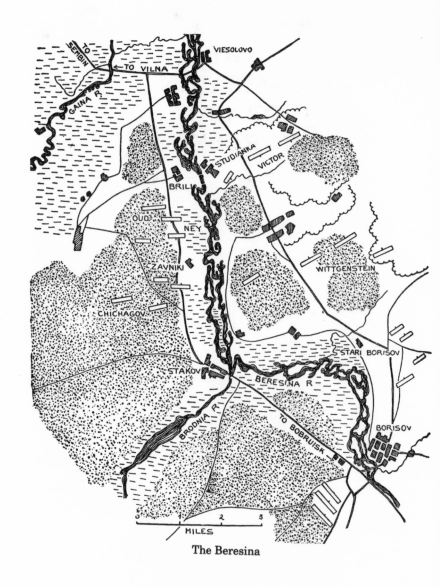

TO SERBIN
TO VILNA
VIESOLOVO
GAINA R.
STUDIANKA
VICTOR
BRILI
OUDI
NEY
ZAVNIKI
WITTGENSTEIN
CHICHAGOV
STARI BORISOV
STAKOV
BERESINA R.
BRODNIA R.
TO BOBRUISK
BORISOV

0   1   2   3
MILES

The Beresina

THE CAMPAIGN OF 1812 IN RUSSIA

GENERAL
CARL VON CLAUSEWITZ

with a new foreword by
SIR MICHAEL HOWARD

DA CAPO PRESS • NEW YORK

Library of Congress Cataloging in Publication Data

Clausewitz, Carl von, 1780–1831.
  [Feldzug 1812 in Russland. English]
  The campaign of 1812 in Russia / Carl von Clausewitz; foreword
by Michael Howard.—1st Da Capo Press ed.
    p.   cm.
  ISBN 0-306-80650-9 (alk. paper)
  1. Napoleonic Wars, 1800–1815—Campaigns—Russia. 2. Russia—
History, Military—1801–1917. I. Title.
DC235.C6132 1995
940.2'7—dc20   95-15743
                                                                    CIP

First Da Capo Press edition 1995

This Da Capo Press paperback edition of *The Campaign of
1812 in Russia* is an unabridged republication of the edition
published in England in 1843, with the addition of a new
foreword by Sir Michael Howard and maps from *Napoleon* (1907)
by Theodore Ayrault Dodge.

Published by Da Capo Press, Inc.
A Subsidiary of Plenum Publishing Corporation
233 Spring Street, New York, N.Y. 10013

Manufactured in the United States of America

FOREWORD

ALTHOUGH Clausewitz wrote histories of all the major Napoleonic campaigns, his account of the invasion of Russia in 1812 is of peculiar interest. This is not merely because of the account Clausewitz gives of Napoleon's strategy and tactics. Indeed for the military analyst the campaign itself, consisting as it did of a straightforward advance and retreat and involving only one major battle conducted with little finesse on either side, is not a very rewarding object for detailed study, decisive though it was in the history of Europe. Clausewitz has no difficulty in giving a comprehensive chronicle of it in a single chapter of this book. No, the real interest of the work lies in the part that was played in the campaign by Clausewitz himself, and his firsthand observations about the events that he witnessed in the course of it.

Leaving aside his youthful participation in the indecisive operations of the War of the First Coalition from 1793 to 1796, Karl von Clausewitz was involved in four major campaigns of the Napoleonic Wars: that of Jena in 1806; that of 1812, chronicled here; the confused fighting in the wars of Liberation of 1813-14; and finally that of

1815, known to the English-speaking world as Waterloo.

In the first of these Clausewitz had been a very junior officer with no involvement in strategic or tactical decisions. In the last, although he was Chief of Staff to an army corps, his unit played only a peripheral role in the climactic battles. In 1812, however, he was close to, and often part of, the Russian Headquarters Staff throughout the major part of the campaign, and a witness to all its major decisions. When towards the end of the year he was detached to a subordinate theater in the north, he there found himself able to play a key role in one of the most significant events, not only of the campaign itself, but in the entire history of Prussia and of Europe as a whole—the negotiation and signing of the Convention of Tauroggen, whereby the commander of the Prussian forces serving under French command, General Yorck von Wartenburg, abandoned his French allies and thus enabled the King of Prussia to establish himself as the leader of a new German War of Liberation against the Napoleonic Empire. The book therefore should be read, not simply as a history and analysis of the military campaign, but as a chapter of autobiography and an eyewitness account of what proved to be a turning-point in European political as well as military history.

Although the final text was published only posthumously in the comprehensive edition of his collected works that appeared between 1832 and

1837, Clausewitz appears to have written most of it within a year or two of the event itself. Certainly the narrative bears all the imprint of immediacy. But although Clausewitz gives us a full account of his experiences from his arrival at the Russian Imperial Headquarters on the eve of the campaign in May 1812 until the conclusion of the Convention of Tauroggen the following December, he does not explain how it was that he, a Prussian officer, came to be with the Russian armies at a time when his own country was fighting in alliance with Napoleon against the Russian Empire. A few words of explanation are therefore necessary.

Karl von Clausewitz was born in 1780 and had served with the Prussian Army from the age of twelve. As a young staff officer, he became a leading member of the group of military reformers led by Gerhard von Scharnhorst, whose attempts to reform the Prussian Army had no time to bear fruit before its catastrophic defeat at the hand of Napoleon in the Jena campaign of 1806. Thereafter Clausewitz was one of those urging King Frederick William III of Prussia to introduce the political reforms that would be a necessary preliminary to the military reforms needed to re-establish Prussia as a major European power. A combination of political conservatism and timidity in the face of virtual occupation by the Napoleonic armies made the Prussian monarch regard such advice as unwelcome, if not downright impractical. Clausewitz's marriage to a favorite lady-in-waiting of the Queen gave him a certain freedom of expression, but the conservative advisers of the King continued to regard him not as a patriot but as a dangerously subversive liberal.

When in the spring of 1812 Prussia was compelled to enter into a formal alliance with Napoleon in preparation for the latter's intended campaign against Russia, Clausewitz could bear no more. Rather than endure the humiliation of fighting under the command of Prussia's conquerors, he preferred, like many of his countrymen, to join the ranks of her formal enemies. Ironically enough the same conflict of loyalties was to be experienced a century or so later by the French themselves, when they were in their turn defeated by Hitler's Germany and a small number of officers renounced their loyalty to their capitulating government, joining, with Charles de Gaulle, the ranks of the Allies. Like de Gaulle, Clausewitz believed that the true interests of his country could lie only in the defeat and humiliation of its conqueror, and that the best way he could serve Prussia was to join the ranks of Napoleon's enemies. The King gave Clausewitz permission to leave his service with understandable ill grace, and was never fully to take him back into his favor. Once the war was over Clausewitz was shunted into the dead-end job of Superintendent of the War Academy, where at least he had plenty of leisure to reflect on his experiences and write his great work *On War*.

Thus it was that Clausewitz arrived at Czar Alexander I's headquarters in May 1812. As a close colleague of von Scharnhorst he already had a certain reputation, but his usefulness was severely limited by his inability to speak Russian. Fortunately there was already at least one distinguished Prussian officer in the Czar's service, General Karl Ludwig von Phull, so Alexander initially appointed Clausewitz to the latter's staff.

From this point the book speaks for itself. We can read Clausewitz's own assessment of the disastrous von Phull, as of the other senior officers in Alexander's entourage. His study of Kutuzov, the victorious commander of the Russian armies, is of particular interest. Here was a man apparently indecisive, barely even attempting to impose his will on events. "He appeared," wrote Clausewitz, "destitute of inward activity, of any clear view of surrounding occurrences, of any liveliness of perception, or independence of action. He suffered the subordinate directors of the contest to take their own course, and appeared to be for the individual transactions of the day nothing but an abstract idea of central authority" (p. 141). Yet Kutuzov proved to possess a remarkable insight into the inwardness of events, and a genius for exploiting their appearance to his advantage, using such slender evidence as there was on hand to give an appearance of con-

fidence that sustained the morale of his army
and the Russian people through the darkest days
until that of Napoleon himself collapsed.

Once he had taken the prudent decision to
withdraw his main forces into the interior, the
Emperor himself left for Moscow. Clausewitz remained attached to the rearguard of the army, a
close and critical observer of events whose out-
come he did not have the influence, or the lin-
guistic capacity, to affect. But of the overall
Russian strategy of withdrawing into the interior, he thoroughly approved. He observed how
the French were exhausting themselves even by
their very success, losing more men by sickness
or desertion every step of the way. Each stage of
the Russian retreat, on the other hand, provided
their own armies with further strength.
Clausewitz described how they found in all the
chief provincial towns "magazines of flour, grits,
biscuit, and meat; in addition to these, enormous
caravans arrived from the interior with provisions, shoes, leather, and other necessaries: they
had also at their command a mass of carriages,
the teams of which were subsisted without difficulty, since corn and oats were on the ground,
and the caravans of the country are accustomed,
even in time of peace, to pasture their draft cattle in the meadows" (p. 175). He watched the
burning of Moscow, adding his voice to those who
maintained that it was purely accidental. Once
winter set in and the French began to retreat,
Clausewitz briefly but vividly described the hard-

ships of the campaign, from which he himself suffered severely and was never fully to recover. He was so badly affected by frostbite that his face remained reddened for the rest of his life, giving rise to the rumor that he was a secret drinker.

The experience of this campaign was to provide Clausewitz with a rich store of data on which he drew when he came to write *On War*. Those familiar with that work will recognize in *The Campaign of 1812* many of the ideas that were to be fully worked out in that comprehensive study. For example, we find here Clausewitz's recognition of the limited contribution that the military theorist can bring to the actual conduct of operations. "The man who means to move in such a medium as the element of war," he writes, "should bring with him nothing from books but the general education of his understanding. If he extract from them, on the contrary, ideas cut and dried, not derived from the impulse of the moment, the stream of events will dash his structure to the ground before it is finished. He will never be intelligible to others, men of natural genius; and least of all in the most distinguished among them, those who know their own wishes and intentions, will they inspire confidence" (p. 41).

Further, it was during the course of this campaign that he formulated his famous paradox "that the offensive form is the weaker, and the defensive the stronger, in war; but that the results of the first, when successful, are positive, therefore the greater and more decisive; of the latter only negative, by which the equilibrium is restored" (p. 120). He noted the reluctance of his Russian allies to believe anything of the kind, believing as they did that "the Russian soldier is more adapted for the attack than the defence. It is known," added Clausewitz drily, "that all armies assert this of themselves" (p. 115).

We further find, arising out of his close involvement in the Battle of Borodino, Clausewitz's equally unpopular but profoundly influential conclusion that battles are won rather by attrition, the slow exhaustion of reserves, than by either the skillful maneuvers beloved of military theorists or the "shock" so dear to the hearts of fighting soldiers. This insight was to be rediscovered, rather disastrously, by commanders on both sides of the Western Front in the First World War. And he shares his insight that the principal difficulty facing a commander will always lie in the overcoming of the *inertia* of the forces under his command, especially when he is urging his forces to pursuit after a successful battle. In replying to those who criticized Kutuzov for not totally destroying the Napoleonic armies on their retreat, he advises them that if they "reflect on the winter in all its inhospitality, on shattered powers, physical and moral, an army led from bivouac to bivouac, suffering from privation, decimated by sickness, its path strewn with dead, dying and exhausted bodies—they will comprehend with what difficulty each motion was accomplished, and how nothing but the strongest impulses could overcome the exhaustion of the mass" (p. 212).

Perhaps indeed the most important lesson that Clausewitz learned from this and his other campaigns was the importance of "friction" in war, and we find here, already fully minted, one of the central concepts of *On War*.

In war all is simple; but the most simple is still very difficult. The instrument of war resembles a machine with prodigious friction, which cannot, as in ordinary mechanics, be adjusted at pleasure, but is ever in contact with a host of chances. War is, moreover, a movement through a dense medium. A motion easy in air is difficult in water. Toil and danger are the elements in which the mind has to act in war, and of these elements we know nothing in the closet. It thus falls out that we remain behind the line that we have drawn by anticipation, and that no common powers are required to maintain us even at a medium point [p. 185].

In his final analysis of the campaign, as in all his military writings and analysis, Clausewitz grounded his judgments firmly on his appreciation of what, under the circumstances, was and was not possible, on what could and could not be done with armies. Napoleon's strategy in 1812, he grants, was a gamble; but it was the same kind of gamble that had paid off handsomely in all his previous campaigns. He failed not so much because of any military errors as because of a political miscalculation—a miscalculation very similar to that made by Hitler a century later. Napoleon believed that if he defeated the

Russian army and occupied Moscow, the Russian leadership would fall apart and the government would be compelled to sue for peace. But the Russian army, although badly battered, did not admit that it was defeated. The occupation of Moscow did not lead to the disintegration of the Russian government. Having staked all, according to his usual practice, on a single throw, Napoleon had no resources left to stave off disaster. Clausewitz criticizes him for paying so little attention to logistics that the French armies were already exhausted by the time they arrived at Moscow, suggesting that if only Napoleon had remained "formidable" even after the acquisition of Moscow things might have turned out differently. But he does not fault his overall strategy. It was too much part of the man; and once he had decided to launch such a campaign, boldness was probably wiser than caution. "He owed everything to his boldness of interpretation," concludes Clausewitz, "and his most brilliant campaigns would have been exposed to the same imputations as have attached to the one we have described, if they had not succeeded" (p. 260). It was this magisterial fairness of judgment, rooted in experience rather than in abstraction, that placed Clausewitz, as a military analyst, in a class by himself, and which has made his teaching continually relevant to the conduct of war.

SIR MICHAEL HOWARD
March 1995

CONTENTS

THE MAPS

Maps from *Napoleon* (1907)
by Theodore Ayrault Dodge

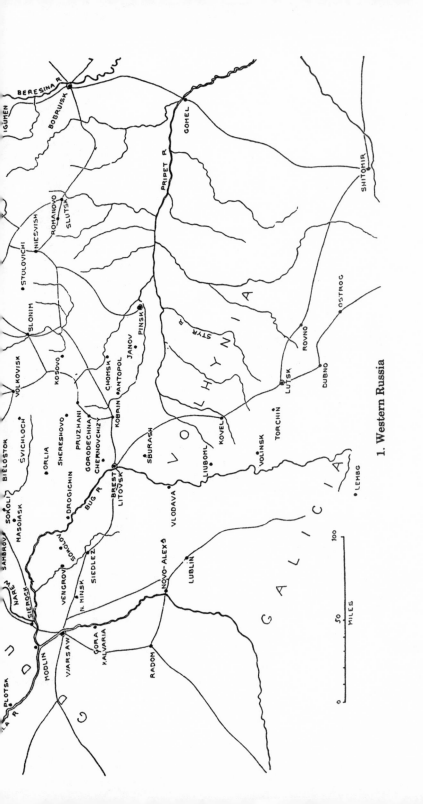

1. Western Russia

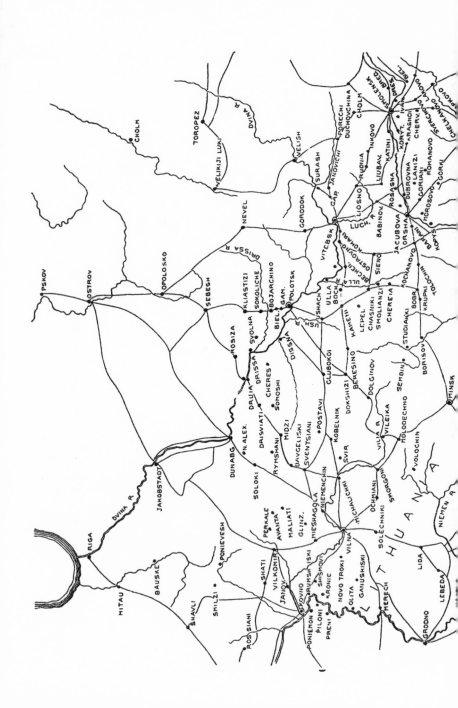

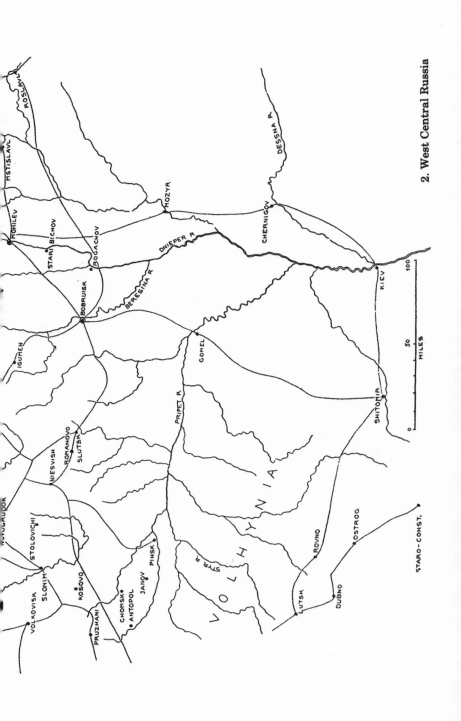

2. West Central Russia

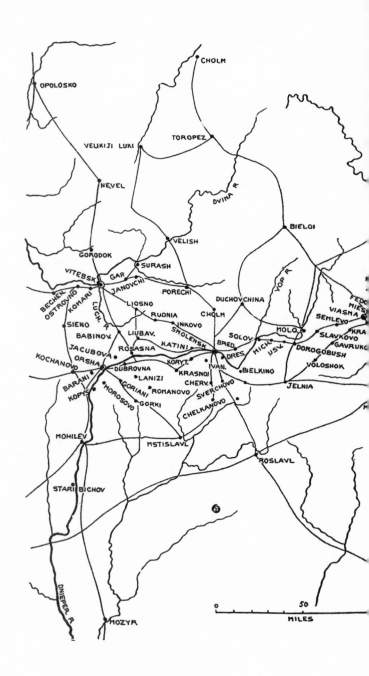

TVER

VOLGA R

DIMITROV

SUBZOV

VOLOKOLAMSK

VOSKRESENSK

POKROV

RUSA

SVENIGROD

BOGORODSK

MOSCOW

PAVLOVO

GSHASK

GRID.

BORODINO

KOL.

SLOBODA

MOZHAISK

JELNIA

PACHRA R

KROV

R SAIM

ER.

TATARIKINO

VELISHEVO

SPASKOI

VEREIA

PODOLSK

BRONIZI

MAXIMOVO

AIA

SILENKI

DUBROVNA

BOROVSK

TARUTINO

KOLOMNA

MEDINI

USHA R

HALO.

NARA R

PROTVA R

OKA R

JUKNOV

SALSK

KALUGA

RIASAN

TULA

DON R

100

OREL

3. East Central Russia

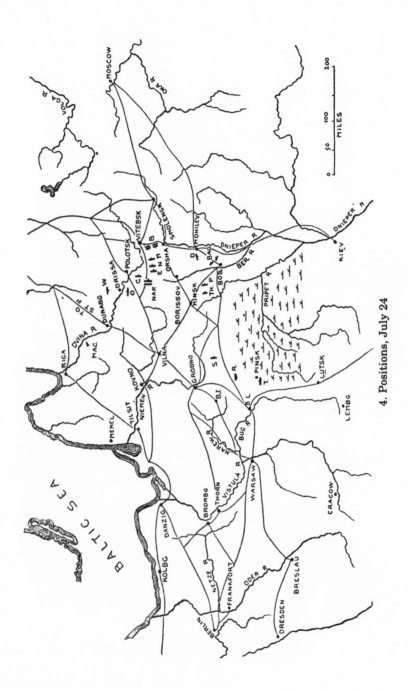

4. Positions, July 24

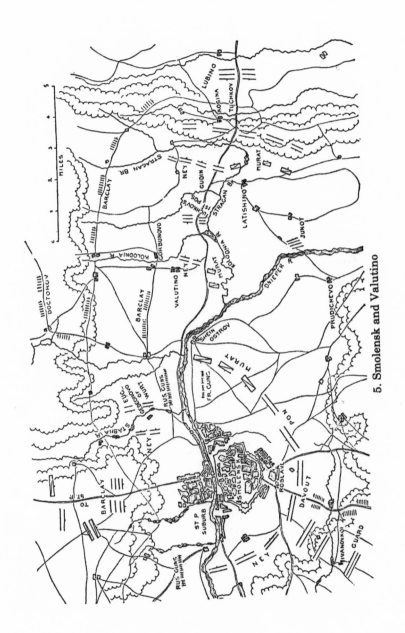

5. Smolensk and Valutino

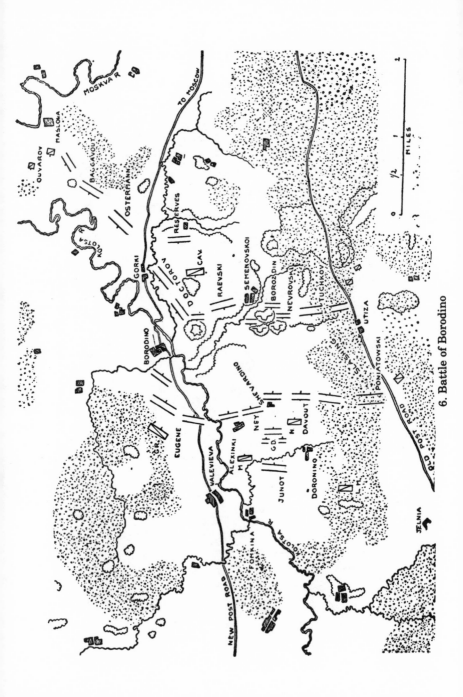

6. Battle of Borodino

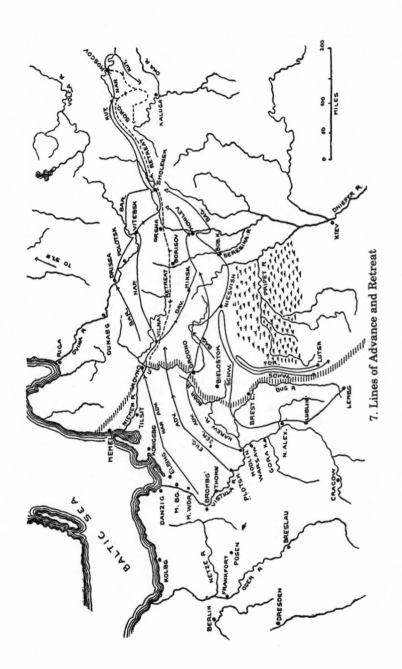

7. Lines of Advance and Retreat

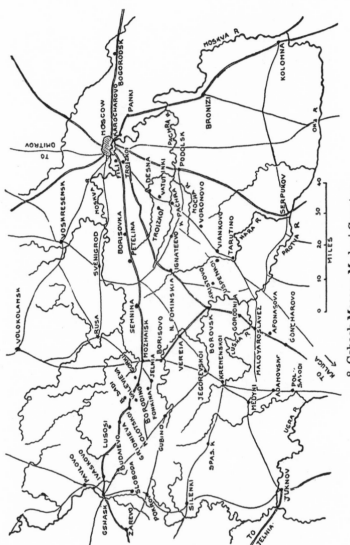

8. Gshask-Moscow-Medyni Country

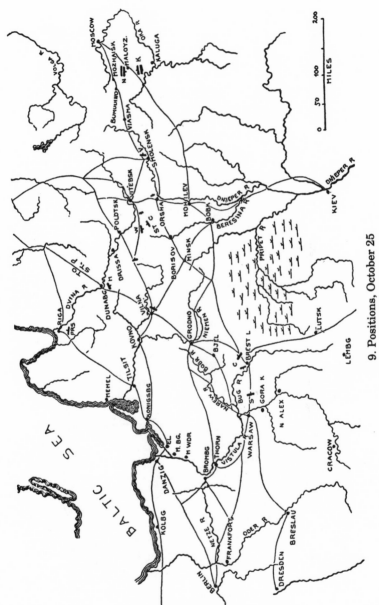

9. Positions, October 25

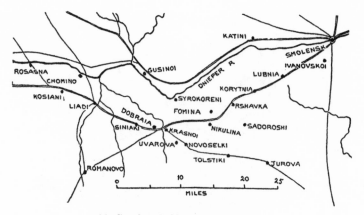

10. Smolensk-Krasnoi Country

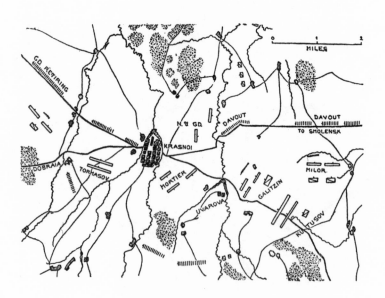

11. Battle of Krasnoi

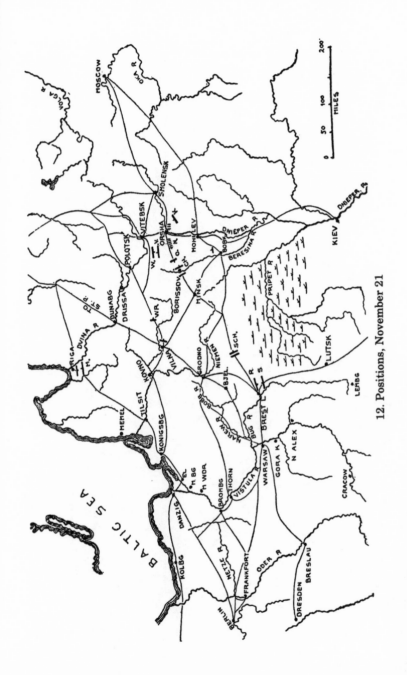

12. Positions, November 21

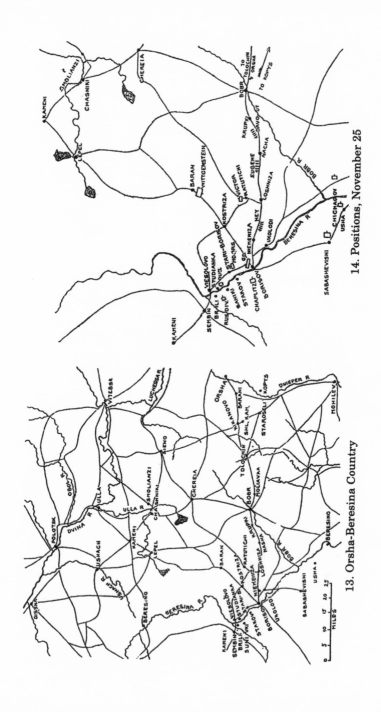

14. Positions, November 25

13. Orsha-Beresina Country

RUSSIAN CAMPAIGN

OF 1812.

CHAPTER I.

ARRIVAL AT WILNA. PLAN OF CAMPAIGN. CAMP
OF DRISSA.

IN February of 1812, the alliance between France
and Prussia against Russia was concluded.   The
party in Prussia, which still felt courage to resist,
and refused to acknowledge the necessity of a
junction with France, might properly be called the
Scharnhorst party; for in the capital, besides himself and his near friends, there was hardly a man
who did not set down this temper of mind for a
semi-madness.   In the rest of the monarchy nothing
but a few scattered indications of such a spirit
were to be found.

So soon as this alliance was an ascertained fact,
Scharnhorst quitted the centre of government, and
betook himself to Silesia, where, as inspector of
fortresses, he reserved to himself a sort of official
activity.   He wished at once to withdraw himself
from the observation of the French, and from an

active co-operation with them, utterly uncongenial
to his nature, without entirely giving up his relations to the Prussian service.   This half measure
was one of eminent prudence.   He was able, in his
present position, to prevent much mischief, par-
ticularly as regarded concessions to France in the
matter of the Prussian fortresses, and he kept his
foot in the stirrup, ready to swing himself into the
saddle at the favourable moment.   He was a
foreigner, without possessions or footing in Prussia,
had always remained a little estranged from the
King, and more so from the leading personages of
the capital ; and the merit of his operations was
generally at this time much exposed to question.
If he had now entirely abandoned the service, it
may be questioned whether he would have been
recalled to it in 1813.

The Major Von Boyen, his intimate friend, who
had held the function of personal communication
with the King on military affairs, now obtained
his congé, carrying with him the rank of Colonel
and a small donation. It was his intention to go
to Russia.   The Colonel Von Gneisenau, lately
made state councillor, left the service at the same
time, with a like intention.

Several others among the warmest adherents of
Scharnhorst, and of his political views, but who
were of small importance in the state, did the same ;
among whom was the Author. The King granted
their congé to all.

The Author, provided with some letters of

recommendation, went to Wilna, then the head-quarters of the Emperor Alexander, as also of the General Barclay, who commanded the 1st army of the West.

On the Author's arrival at Wilna, he found several Prussian officers already there assembled. Among those of consequence were Gneisenau and Count Chasot, who had made the journey from Vienna in company. The former had already however resolved on a journey to England. He had indeed been well received by the Emperor, but had come to the conclusion, from the whole appearance of things, that he could find in Russia no fitting theatre for the active exercise of his profession. He understood no Russian, and could therefore fill no independent command : he was too far advanced in years and rank to allow of his being introduced into some subordinate station on the staff of any general or any corps, like the Author or other officers ; he could therefore only have made the campaign in the suite of the Emperor. He knew well what this involved, or rather did not involve, and he felt that it opened no prospect worthy of his talents. The head-quarters of the Emperor were already overrun with distinguished idlers. To attain either distinction or usefulness in such a crowd would have required the dexterity of an accomplished intriguer, and an entire familiarity with the French language : in both he was deficient. He was therefore justly averse to the seeking a position in Russia ; and he hoped in

England*, where he had already travelled, and had been well received by the Prince Regent, to do much more for the good cause.

As he had soon convinced himself in Wilna that the measures of Russia were anything but adequate to the emergency, he justly entertained the greatest apprehensions for the consequences, and believed that his only hope lay in the difficulty of the entire enterprise on the part of France, but that every thing should be done to effect on the side of England, Sweden, and Germany, a diversion on the rear of the French. This view derived force from his visit to England.

The whole force of Russia, on the western frontier, consisted of the 1st and 2d armies of the West, and an army of reserve. The first might be 90,000 strong, the second 50,000, and the third 30,000. The whole therefore amounted to some 170,000 men, to whom may be added 10,000 Cossacks.

The 1st army, under General Barclay, who at the same time was war minister, was placed along the Niemen; the second, commanded by Bagration, in south Lithuania, the reserve under Tormasow, in Volhynia. On the second line there were about 30,000 men of depôts and recruits, on the Dnieper and Dwina.

The Emperor wished to take the command of the

---

* He had visited England without ostensible functions, but really on a mission from his government, in 1806.—T.

whole : he had never served in the field, still less commanded. For several years past he had taken lessons in the art of war from Lieutenant-General Von Phull in Petersburgh.

Phull had held the rank of Colonel on the general staff of the Prussian army, and in 1806, after the battle of Auerstadt, had left the Prussian service and entered that of Russia, in which he had since obtained the rank of Lieutenant-General without having passed through any active service.

Phull passed in Prussia for a man of much genius. He, Massenbach, and Scharnhorst, were the three chiefs of the Prussian staff in 1806. Each of these had his own peculiarities of character. Those of Scharnhorst alone had proved themselves practically available ; those of Phull were perhaps the most unusual, but very difficult to characterise. He was a man of much understanding and cultivation, but without a knowledge of actual things: he had, from the earliest period, led a life so secluded and contemplative, that he knew nothing of the occurrences of the daily world ; Julius Cæsar and Frederick the Great were the heroes and the writers of his predilection. The more recent phenomena of war passed over him without impression. In this way he had framed for himself a one-sided and meagre system of war, which could stand the test neither of philosophical investigation, nor historical comparison. If in the mode of his intellectual cultivation historical criticism was deficient, and in his way of life all contact with the external world, it on the other hand was natural that he should become an enemy to all ordinary superficiality, falsehood, and weakness ; and the bitter irony with which he broke out against these common failings of the many gave him especially the appearance of greater geniality, depth, and power. Seclusion had rendered him an isolated being ; but being free from eccentricity of manner, he did not pass for such.

With all this, the straight-forward direction of the man, his inward truth, his abhorrence for falsehood and meanness, and his lively sentiment for the great, would have made of him a distinguished character, and one even available for the path of military eminence, if his mind, unfamiliarised with the phenomena of the external world, had not become confused so soon as they pressed upon his attention. The author never saw a man who lost his head so easily, who, intent as he ever was on great things, was so soon overwhelmed by the least of little realities. This was the natural result of his secluded self-education. Yielding and pliable by nature, he had reasoned himself into a certain grandeur of views and strength of resolution, which were not natural to him, and, separated from the external world, he had foregone all opportunity of training himself by conflict with it to this assumed character. Up to the period of 1812, the incidents of service had not impelled him to this exercise. In the war of the Revolution he had played generally a subordinate part; and it had been only towards the end of hostilities that he had assumed a more important post as quarter-master-general to Field Marshal Mollendorf. During the years of peace attached to the general staff, he found himself, like most officers of that department, in a sort of illusory activity, which exercises itself in mere ideas.

In the year 1806 he was officer of the general staff of the King; but as the King did not command, Phull was not in personal activity as such. After the entire catastrophe, his irony broke loose on every thing which had happened. He laughed like a madman at the defeat of the army; and instead of coming forward at a moment when a vacancy of consequence had occurred in the ranks, as Scharnhorst did, to show his practical efficiency, and to piece up new threads to those which yet remained sound in the lacerated texture, he gave up every thing for lost, and took service with Russia.

He gave in this manner the first proof that he had no practical vocation for difficulties. He managed his transfer also with great want of address, by accepting a foreign service in Petersburgh at a moment when he was employed there on a mission.

Had the Emperor Alexander possessed more knowledge of mankind, he would naturally have conceived little confidence in the abilities of a man who gave up a failing cause so early and conducted himself at the same time with so little dexterity.

In Mollendorf's head-quarters at Hochheim in 1797, Phull said, " I trouble myself now about nothing, for everything is going to the devil. " In the year 1806 he said on his flight, taking off his hat, " Adieu the Prussian monarchy." In November, 1812, at Petersburgh, after the French army had begun its retreat, he said to the Author, " Believe me, no good can come of all this." He remained always like himself.

The Author has dwelt thus long on the character of this man, because, as will presently appear, much that occurred was connected with his appearance on the stage, and, subsequently, a still greater share in events has been attributed to him than his peculiarities admitted of his assuming.

If we have passed a sentence little to his advantage on his mind and understanding, to the honour of his integrity we must say that no better heart, no more disinterested character could be imagined than he on every occasion displayed.

Unpractical as he was, in six years of residence in Russia he had not thought of learning Russian, nor, which is more striking, had he thought of making himself acquainted with the principal persons in the administration of affairs, or with the institutions of the civil and military departments.

The Emperor * felt that under these circumstances Phull was to be considered as an abstract

---

* The Author here appears scarcely consistent with himself. It is clear from his subsequent narrative, that, up to a critical period of the campaign, the fortunes of the Russian army and empire were staked on a plan of this abstract genius, which the force of circumstances alone compelled the Emperor to abandon before it was too late to do so.—T.

genius, to whom no particular function could be assigned. He was therefore nothing more than friend and adviser to the Emperor *pro formâ,* also his adjutant-general. He had already in St. Petersburgh drawn out a plan of campaign for the Emperor, which was now brought to Wilna, and some measures were adopted towards its execution.

The prince Wolkonski.—He was first adjutant-general to the Emperor, and administrative chief of the general staff. In this capacity, so soon as the Emperor should have taken the command, he might have considered himself as *de facto* chief of the staff for the whole war: this, however, did not so turn out, and he took as good as no share at all in these affairs. He was a well-humoured man, and true friend and servant of the Emperor.

The Lieut.-General Aractschejef.*—A Russian, in every sense of the word, of great energy and cunning. He was chief of the artillery, and the Emperor had great confidence in him; the conduct however of a war being a thing quite strange to him, he mixed himself up in it just as little as did Wolkonski.

The General Arenfeld.—The well-known Swede, who has always passed for a great intriguer. The conduct of war on a large scale seemed strange to him also; and he therefore sought no kind of active position, but contented himself, like Phull, with the

---

* Afterwards conspicuous as the prime mover and agent of the Emperor in the establishment of the Russian military colonies.—T.

title of an adjutant-general, but was inclined to mix himself in intrigues.

The General Benningsen.—He was one of the oldest generals of the Russian army, at the moment however called to no command, probably because his ill success in 1807 was remembered. He was at Wilna under pretext of mere courtesy, because his estates lay in that vicinity, and, as adjutant-general to the Emperor, he could not remain absent: he was striving however for a command.

The remaining military personages, among whom figured indeed many a lieutenant-general, were still more insignificant, and entirely without influence on the operations of the war.

We discern from this how little the Emperor had prepared himself for the actual command. He himself, it would seem, never entertained this idea distinctly, nor formally expressed it. The two armies were for the moment separated, while, as war minister, Barclay held some control over the second; the idea then of a command-in-chief resided in him alone and his staff. He had a chief of the general staff in Lieut.-General Labanow, a quarter-master-general in General Mouchin, an intendant-general, &c. All these personages had entered on the functions of their respective posts. The General Barclay issued daily his orders, received the reports and announcements, &c. None of this took place regularly with the Emperor. Most of the orders given passed through Barclay, some through Wolkonski, and perhaps Phull might once or twice put in his oar.

When the Emperor reached Wilna, with Phull in his suite, the latter found himself isolated—a stranger among Russians, who looked upon him with envy, disfavour, and distrust. He knew neither the language, the persons, nor the institutions of the country and army: he had no place, no kind of authority, no aide-de-camps, no bureau; he received no reports, no communications. He was not in the most distant connection with Barclay or any body else; he never interchanged words with any. What he knew of the strength and condition of the army he had heard from the Emperor. He was in possession of no one complete statement of numbers, or other documents, the study of which is essential to the consideration of the preliminaries of a campaign. In his memoranda he was often at a loss for the names of the commanders of whom he wished to speak, and was obliged to help himself out by describing the positions they occupied.

An inconceivable degree of folly was required for a man in such circumstances to undertake the conduct of a great transaction of war, involving such difficulties as might be foreseen in the case of the approaching campaign. The Russian army was 180,000 strong, if taken at a high estimate; the enemy, at the lowest, 350,000, and Buonaparte their leader.

Phull should have dissuaded the Emperor from the idea of the chief command, or endeavoured to

forward other arrangements. He did neither the
one nor the other, but acted like the sleep-walker,
who walks the roof of the house securely, and
wakes to fall and be destroyed.

At the very moment when the Russian army on
the frontier did not count above 180,000 men, it
was asserted that the Emperor had 600,000 men in
pay; and this assertion, which the Author at first
considered as a sarcastic exaggeration, although
received from the mouth of an *employé* of rank,
was the simple truth.

The distribution of the Russian force really on
foot was as follows:—

On the frontier towards Poland and Prussia	180,000 men.
On the Dwina and Dnieper, depôts and new formations	30,000
In Finland	20,000
In Moldavia	60,000
Eastern frontiers	30,000
Interior, new levies and depôts	50,000
Garrisons	50,000
	420,000

The Cossacks are not here reckoned. If we add
this great swarm, which, however, at the opening
of the war did not exceed 10,000 men, with the
western army, and at no period exceeded 20,000—if
we add other militants of smaller account, and
consider how many misusages have obtained a
half prescription in the Russian army, and how
great, then, must be the difference between the
numbers on the pay lists and in the field, we may

conceive how for 420,000 of the latter, the numbers of the former should reach 600,000.

The Russians, in the bygone year, and while preparing for war with France, had not materially increased their army—a proof that they were unable to furnish greater levies. We may assume that, at the moment of the war, the reinforcements may have reached 80,000, which joined the depôts and formed the force which joined on the Dnieper and Dwina, and, later, at Smolensko and Kaluga, and which, exclusive of militia, could not have exceeded 100,000 men.

The result of these reckonings appears, first, that the Russian army's proper effective strength was 600,000 men, and that it probably could not be raised to a higher amount without an undue strain on the resources of the country. Secondly, that in the year 1812 not above 400,000 regular troops were actually forthcoming. Thirdly, that of these 400,000 not more than 180,000 could be opposed, in the first instance, to the French.

This over-valuation of forces is always occurring : one example is afforded by Prussia in 1806, when she payed 250,000 men, and could not oppose to the French, in Thuringia, more than 100,000. Even if we may succeed in devising better arrangements than those of Prussia in 1806, or Russia in 1812, it is yet well sometimes to bring to our recollection these leading instances, in order to avoid similar errors.

In any case Russia was rather behindhand in its

measures, and the peace with Turkey had remained too long unconcluded. Two months later Russia would have been able to appear in the field with 150,000 men more, nearly the double of her present force.

The Emperor and Phull had hit upon the sound idea that the real resistance must begin later and from the interior, on account of their weakness on the frontier. Phull, therefore, proposed to draw back the struggle to a considerable distance, thus approaching their reinforcements, gaining time, weakening the enemy by means of the detachments which he would be compelled to make, and gaining space for strategical operations upon his flank and rear. This project was the better entertained by the Emperor, because it reminded him of Wellington's Portuguese campaign of 1811.

Taken abstractedly, these ideas would seem to involve the whole campaign of 1812 as it occurred. Such, however, is not the fact. Proportion is every thing in war: schemes admirably adapted for effect on a scale of 100 miles, on one of 30 may be utterly deceptive. We cannot so much as say that Phull's idea had supplied the model after which the actual campaign, in its colossal grandeur, was conducted. The campaign, as we shall see, worked out its own form, and Phull's idea has the less pretension to be considered the leading one, as in itself it was a false one. His idea, however, was the accidental cause of the turn which the campaign took, as we shall see.

Phull's plan was, that the first army of the West should withdraw into an entrenched camp, for which he had selected the neighbourhood of the middle Dwina, that the earliest reinforcements should be sent hither, and a great provision of articles of subsistence be accumulated there, and that Bagration with the 2d army of the west should press forward on the right flank and rear of the enemy, should he engage himself in the pursuit of the 1st. Tormasow remained destined to the defence of Volhynia against the Austrians. What were the active principles of this scheme?

1st. Approximation to reinforcements. — The spot selected lay 20 miles from the frontier* ; it was hoped at first to raise the 1st army of the West to 130,000 men, but the reinforcement it obtained was far less than was expected. As the Author was informed, it did not exceed 10,000 men, and the army was therefore about 100,000. The retreat was therefore not sufficiently extended to produce any considerable accession of numbers. This error however of the plan is not to be considered as an error of the original idea. The Emperor may have deceived himself, and, if so, Phull was the more excusable.

2d. The weakening of the enemy on his advance is never considerable on such a distance as the one

---

* It must be remembered that the miles spoken of in this work are German, being to the English as 5 to 1, or nearly. — T.

in question, and when he is not checked by fortresses, and it may here be considered as nothing. *

3d. The attack of Bagration on the flank and rear
of the enemy is not to be considered as a valid
feature. If this army was to fight the enemy from
behind, it could not do so from before, and the
French had only to oppose to it a proportionate
mass of troops, in order to restore the balance,
by which the advantage would remain to them of
finding themselves between our armies, and able to
fall on either of them with an overwhelming force.

Strategical operations on a hostile flank are to be
considered as available modes of action, when the
enemy's line of operations is greatly extended
through hostile provinces, and requires detachments
for its security, which weaken the main body.
Such was the case in 1812, when the French had
pressed forward to Moscow, but were not properly
masters of the country right and left, further than
the Dnieper and the Dwina.

Flanking operations are also available when the
hostile army is so far at the extreme circumference
of its circle of action, that it can no longer turn a
victory to account over the force in its front, and
this latter may therefore be weakened without
danger. Finally, when the result is decided, and
all that remains is to embarrass the retreat, as in

* As matter of previous calculation, perhaps, but from accidental circumstances, Buonaparte's loss within the first 100
miles (English) from the frontier, was in fact very great.—T.

the case of Tschitshagow's attack on the rear of Buonaparte in 1812.

In no other case is anything accomplished by the mere turning of a flank. On the contrary, this measure, as one leading to greater and more decided results, is also, of necessity, one of greater risk, i. e. one which requires more strength than the parallel form of resistance, and is therefore unsuited to the weaker party. Of all this Phull had never formed a clear conception, as, indeed, few at this time were accustomed to form such in these matters, and every one judged according to his own allowance of tact and discernment.

4th. The entrenched camp.—That, in a strong position, a few may resist many, is well known. But then it is essential that such position should have its rear perfectly free, as in the case of Torres Vedras, or at least should make a complete system of defence by connection with a neighbouring fortress, such as the camp of Bunzelwitz in the Seven Years' War, and thus avoid the risk of being starved.

The position chosen for the Russian camp was near Drissa, on the Dwina. Phull, in Petersburgh, had induced the Emperor to dispatch the Colonel Wolzogen, an officer of talent and instruction, who before 1806 had left the Prussian for the Russian service, with instructions to select the spot for such a camp. We know nothing of his particular instructions. The result was, that in this district, singularly barren of military positions, he succeeded in finding no other point than that of

Drissa, where a wooded surface of limited extent, partly covered by morasses, afforded space for a camp with its rear leaning on the Dwina. Its advantages were, that the river forms here a concave semicircle, of which the chord is about a league. In front of this chord was extended the front of the camp in a slight curve, and supported on either side by the river, which runs here between banks, only of sand indeed, but fifty feet in height. On the right bank of the Dwina, above and below the flanks of the camp, several minor streams, of which the Drissa is the most considerable, discharge themselves into the Dwina, and afford occasion for good positions, and a favourable field of battle against an enemy who shall have crossed the river to attack the camp from the rear.

The slight curve which formed the front of the camp was fortified with a triple range of works, closed and open, planned by General Phull himself, and the retreat was to be secured by seven bridges. On the other side the river were no works. As the Dwina is here but an inconsiderable stream, pretty broad, indeed, but shallow enough to be fordable, it is easy to see that the tactical strength of this position was not great. It consisted in the works alone.

In a strategical view things were still worse. Drissa lies between the roads which lead from Wilna on Moscow and Petersburg, but lies therefore not *on* either of them.

The shortest road from Wilna to Petersburg

passes by Druja on the Dwina, thence by Sebesch and Pskow; the shortest to Moscow passes by Witebsk. Drissa lies four miles from the first, and twenty-four from the last.

This undecided feature in the position gave great dissatisfaction at Wilna. No one there knew what to make of such a post. The Author asked General Phull, with regard to its object, which line of retreat he contemplated, that upon Moscow or on St. Petersburg? Phull replied, that must depend upon circumstances. It is plain that there was an absence of clearness and determination; for an alternative of such importance could not be left to the chances of the instant.

As the camp of Drissa was only covered by the river from behind, and on the other side were no entrenchments, not even a defensible spot, but only a range of boarded sheds in which the flour sacks were stored, and as the river presented no obstacle, the army would never have been free from anxiety for its provisions, which were not even protected by favourable features of the neighbouring ground.

The fortified position of Drissa had therefore remained a mere idea—an abstraction, for not one of all its essential requisites was forthcoming. A slight curve upon a plain surface, surrounded with wood at the distance of 800 paces, and leaning on either side on a fordable river, is a bad field of battle. A point, moreover, which does not lie on the direct line of retreat, but is torn out of the system of operations, and left to itself, which leans neither

on the sea, nor on a fortress, nor even on a town,
properly so called (Drissa is a wooden village, and
lay not directly behind the camp, 'but sideways,
and beyond the system of defence) — such a point is
indeed anything but one of strategical value.

We cannot, however, lay on Lieutenant-Colonel
Wolzogen the blame of these defects. General
Phull had prescribed the ground to him; and in
this part of Lithuania we must thank God if we
find a space vacant in the forest large enough for
us to draw up in it a considerable body of men.

The strength, then, of this position, could hardly
be considered as a multiplicator of the Russian
numbers. It was, in fact, a Phullish pastime
of the imagination, and vanished quickly before
the realities of the time. The only good produced by this idea was, that it was the immediate cause of the retreat of the army, at least as
far as the Dwina. It involved no efficient principle
for multiplying the force of the resistance, and no
compensation for the disadvantage of divergence
from the simplest form of resistance and retreat.

The principal persons at head-quarters, such as
Barclay, Benningsen, and Arenfeld, could not see
their way in this plan of campaign, and exerted
themselves to shake the Emperor's confidence in the
plan and its author. A kind of intrigue was commenced, having for its object to persuade the
Emperor to accept a battle in the neighbourhood of
Wilna. It was perhaps imagined that the French
would cross the frontier on as wide a front as that

on which the Russians were spread for its defence,
i. e. from Samogitia to Volhynia; and in that case
it might be hoped, that too great a preponderance
of force would not be thrown on the point of Wilna.
The idea of a battle could only be accounted for by
supposing it founded on this absurd calculation.

Thus there arose at Wilna a conflict of opinions,
which at least shook the Emperor's confidence in
the plan of Phull.

At this juncture, Lieutenant-Colonel Wolzogen
arrived at Wilna, having served during the interval
as chief of the staff to the corps of General Essen.
He was master of the Russian language, and better
acquainted than Phull with the principal persons.
He determined to seek for an appointment about
Barclay, with the view of becoming, in some mea-
sure, a link of communication between him and
Phull. He induced the latter to ask of the
Emperor the services of an officer for the establishment of a small bureau. His choice fell on the
Author. The Author received an order to travel to
Drissa, to see how far the works had made progress
and at the same time to fix on the fitting halting-
places for the march. He departed, attended by a
Russian feldjäger, on the twenty-third of June.
When he arrived at Drissa, the officer in command
of the works there took the greatest pleasure in
considering him as a spy, because he had nothing
more to show than an order written in French by
General Phull, and General Phull was not considered as an authority. The Author. however,

succeeded in allaying this mistrust, and he received permission to view the camp. ' This incident showed the Author what he had always apprehended — that Phull would derive from his position nothing but the most humiliating embarrassments, and occasion much danger and confusion.

The Author found the works of the camp traced on a system devised by General Phull himself. The outer circle was formed of a line of embrasures for musquetry; some 50 or 60 paces back was a line of works alternately open and closed. The former were intended for the batteries, the latter for single battalions who were to protect the batteries. Some 500 or 600 paces behind this enceinte was a second range of works, entirely closed, which was considered as a reserve position; in the centre, and in the third line, was a still greater entrenched work, as a kind of redoubt to cover a retreat.

Although this system of fortification was evidently too artificial, the number of works too great, and the whole deficient in a practical view, yet the defence of it with a considerable mass of men, and with the known valour of the Russians, promised a serious resistance. One may even maintain with confidence that the French, if they had chosen to attack this camp by its front, would have consumed their force without gaining their object.

The profile of the works was good, the ground however sandy; and as no external devices for strengthening had as yet been resorted to, palisades, felled trees, wolfs'-holes, &c., there was much to be desired on this side. The Author induced the staff-officer who conducted the works, to think of these appliances, and to set about their immediate preparation.

Of the seven intended bridges not one was yet ready; and as practice and knowledge in this department were wanting to the officer employed, he confessed to the Author his embarrassment, and that he did not know how to deal with the very unequal size of the casks which had been furnished him for this service. The Author pointed out some of the devices usually resorted to in such cases, and promised to suggest the sending of an engineer officer to superintend and conduct these labours.

The most striking defect of the camp of Drissa appeared to the Author, while on the spot, the total want of a fortress on the right bank of the Dwina. The little town of Drissa lay opposite the point of support of the left wing, but built, as it is, of wood without walls, afforded no means of defence. In rear of the bridges no defensible object whatever was to be found. The provisions, which principally consisted of flour in enormous quantities, stowed in sacks, were piled up under mere sheds without side walls, and might as easily be set on fire as destroyed by weather.

Phull's idea was this:—To leave in the entrenchment 50,000 men, out of the 120,000 he hoped to muster, as a sufficient garrison, and with the remaining 70,000 to advance against the enemy, who should have crossed the river to attack the camp from behind.

Should the enemy cross in considerable force and thus weaken himself too much on the left bank, Phull intended to break out of the camp with overpowering numbers and attack the weakened portion. The whole advantage, therefore, of the camp, would consist in its affording an easier and shorter connection between the two sides of the river, while the enemy would be compelled to communicate between the two parts of his army by a single bridge at some distance. This advantage was incontestably of no very decisive character; it was not one which could be relied on to secure the results of a battle between 120,000 men deprived of all means of retreat, and a superior force. It should also have been a condition of such an offensive movement as was contemplated, that the ground should be favourable on the one side of the river or the other: this however was not the case in the front of the position on the left bank, where the ground was so beset with wood and morass, as to allow no view of the enemy's movement. In any case, also, a certain degree of defensive strength was essential on the right bank, if an offensive movement was intended on the left, in order that a small corps might be sufficient to protect the magazines ; this however was not the case, for the neighbouring ground was even, and no trace of fortification apparent. Had the Russians not abandoned this position, their numbers, whether 90,000

or 120,000, could have made no difference — they
must, attacked from behind, have been driven into
the half circle of their fortifications, and compelled
to capitulate.

Phull had adhered to this idea of an entrenched
camp, because in his one-sided mind he could
imagine nothing better.　A battle in the field promised little under the existing disproportion of
numbers: his object, therefore, was to redress the
balance by arrangement and concentration of his
means of defence ; as, however, often happens in
strategical manœuvre, he failed to probe to the
bottom the causes from which he hoped for effects,
and was conducting the Russians to a more destructive and rapid catastrophe, by leaving the
simple path of a direct resistance for one more tor-
tuous, without incorporating into his system any
new principle of defence.　It was only the excess
of his weakness and incapacity which, by causing
his extinction before the catastrophe could be
worked out, saved the Russian army from destruction.

The Author, on his return (June 28.), found the
Imperial head-quarters transferred to Swanziani,
three marches from Wilna.　The war had broken
out, the army had commenced its retreat.　The
head-quarters of General Barclay were two marches
nearer to Wilna.

The Author had now to make his report to the
Emperor of the state in which he had found things
at Drissa.　General Phull was naturally present

on this occasion. The task, as may be imagined, was no easy one: what he had to say against the camp struck directly at General Phull's main measure, and at himself. The Author was at this period the adjutant of that officer; he had been received by him at Wilna in the most friendly manner, and recommended by him to the Emperor: his commission was not one of general criticism on the camp, but only to report on the state in which he had found the works. On the other hand, the importance of the crisis, the deficiencies and errors which in an enlarged view he had discovered, weighed so heavily on his mind, that he felt the strongest necessity to expose the dangers into which the parties and the cause were being hurried. The Emperor, whose confidence had, as we have seen, been shaken before leaving Wilna, felt on his part the necessity of being re-confirmed by a renewed and unconditional eulogy of the measures adopted. The Author thought over these circumstances, and determined, in his report, which he accompanied with a memoir in writing, to confine himself to the terms of his commission, but to touch also lightly on the difficulties which might be expected to occur. The result of the conference was, that the Emperor conceived fresh suspicion that he might find himself embarked in a transaction which had not been maturely considered. The Prince of Oldenburg, husband of the Grand Duchess, afterwards Queen of Wirtemberg, and brother-in-law to the Emperor, who was at the head-quarters, and was treated with the confidence of a friend by the Emperor, some days subsequently told the Author that the Emperor thought he had perceived that the Author had not disclosed his full opinion; to this the latter replied, that he had only endeavoured to direct attention to the objects of chief import- ance, which were yet to be considered, and that many difficulties yet presented themselves to his imagination, which he concluded must already have suggested themselves to the framers of the scheme, in order not to be surprised by them: the Prince said the Emperor had proposed to himself to speak with the Author alone and distinctly upon this subject. Nothing further came of this conversation, the Emperor having already begun to confer on the subject of Drissa with officers better known to him, who declared their opinions with less reserve.

At this juncture, and when they were drawing near to the camp, the Lieutenant-General Count Lieven arrived at head-quarters. He had been Russian minister in Berlin, and had with much kindness assisted the entrance of the Author into the Russian service: the Author called upon him: Count Lieven shared his views and feelings on the state of military affairs. The idea entertained at Berlin was, that Buonaparte must totally fail, in virtue of the great dimensions of the Russian em- pire, if these should only be brought sufficiently into play, i. e. if its resources were husbanded to the last moment, and no peace accepted on any conditions. This idea was specially put forward by Scharnhorst. Count Lieven was full of it, and naturally spoke in the sense of it' to the Emperor. His expression, one which the Author had before heard him use at Berlin, was, that the first pistol shot must be fired at Smolensko. Although this involved a false idea, for a continuous resistance on the retreat was a very essential feature in such a system of defence, yet the leading idea it contained was truly sound, and could not fail to be beneficial if carried out to the extent of not shrinking from evacuating the whole country as far as Smolensko, and only beginning the war in earnest from that point.

The Author imparted Count Lieven's ideas to General Phull, and endeavoured to lead the latter to embrace a bolder conception than that of his entrenched camp. Phull, however, was of all men the slowest to embrace and appropriate the ideas of others; he maintained that the suggestion was founded on exaggeration, without assigning his own reasons against it.

This conversation revived the despondency of the Author as to the conduct of affairs, a feeling which was much aggravated by daily events.

General Barclay, who commanded the army, and had his head-quarters one march to the rear, followed unwillingly the uncertain hand which directed the course of operations. The enemy did not press him strongly, and this occasioned his halting where, according to the general plan, no halt should have been made. Phull was under the apprehension that the enemy might be beforehand with him in reaching Drissa. The Author was several times sent to General Barclay to hurry him on his retreat; and, although Colonel Wolzogen was there, and acted the part of mediator, was always ill received. The Russian rear-guard had the advantage, in several affairs, with the French advanced troops: this gave the troops and their leaders a certain confidence; and General Barclay, a very calm man, feared to impair this spirit by a retreat without resting.

Although the Author did not share the apprehensions of Phull, but considered them proofs of weakness, and therefore went to General Barclay with the greatest reluctance, and though he was pleased with the repose and apparent self-possession of the man, yet this want of obedience and good-will gave him uneasiness. He thought to himself, that it was essential in so immense a transaction for its conductor to be on the spot, to have immediately before him the situation of affairs, their individual position, and to decide only on such grounds. Historical inferences may assist us with ideas for distant objects, when time is allowed to mature them, but cannot enable us to direct armies in the field. On the other hand, opposition and disobedience, at the moment of great transactions, are forerunners of unavoidable destruction.

These reflections presented themselves most forcibly at Vidsky, a town which lies about half way between Wilna and Drissa. While the Em-

peror's head-quarters were there, a report obtained
that the enemy had out-flanked the army on its left,
and that in consequence the order of march must
be altered, unless we wished to see on the morrow
single columns overwhelmed by superior forces.
General Phull, with whom the Author lodged, was
suddenly sent for by the Emperor, and ordered to
bring the Author with him. We found the Emperor in a cabinet. In a larger room without were
the Prince Wolkonski, the General Aractschejef,
Colonel Toll, and the captain of the guard, Count
Orlow. Colonel Toll was of the general staff, and
was soon after quarter-master-general to the army
of Barclay, which, in the Russian service, answers
to the French designation of sous-chef d'état major.
The chief of the general staff was principally concerned with affairs in general; the quarter-master
general specially with the tactical and strategical
details. Although Toll did not hold this post at
the moment, he was in virtual exercise of its
functions.

The Count Orlow was adjutant to Prince
Wolkonski: as however the latter assumed no part
in the direction of the campaign, this young officer
could still less be of weight.

Prince Wolkonski communicated to General
Phull the accounts which had arrived, and told
him the Emperor wished to know what was now to
be done; that as Colonel Clausewitz had selected
the stations for the march towards Drissa, he was
also sent for; and General Phull, with him and

Colonel Toll, was now to consider what was to be done.

General Phull declared at once these were the consequences of General Barclay's disobedience. Prince Wolkonski seemed to admit this, but made the natural observation, that it still remained to decide on their proceedings. Phull here showed himself in his peculiar character. On the one hand thrown into evident perplexity by unexpected occurrences, on the other impelled by long-suppressed bitterness of spirit to the irony which belonged to him, he broke loose with the declaration that as his advice had not been followed, he could not undertake the remedy. While he spoke this, he paced the room up and down.

The Author was at his wits' end with this exhibition. Little soever as he agreed with General Phull, in the eyes of others he was identified with him. Every one considered him a pupil of Phull, engrossed by his ideas, and convinced of his abilities. Phull's behaviour, therefore, was as if it were his own.

Although this humiliating part, which the Author was here, for no fault of his, condemned to play, is but a trifling incident in circumstances of such gravity, he may be pardoned for the excitement which it produced on his own mind. The Prince Wolkonski and General Aractschejef appeared to wait with impatience the upshot of the matter, without the smallest desire on their part to mix themselves in it; at any moment the

Emperor might open his door, and demand the
result of the conference.   Under these circumstances the consultation fell into the hands of the
three younger officers.   Colonel Toll, Count Orlow,
and the Author, laid their heads together to inves-
tigate the matter on the map, spread on a table
before them.   Count Orlow, as a younger officer,
who had never been engaged in the greater movements of war, but was otherwise a man of lively
intelligence, soon fell upon some extraordinary
proposals, which we, the two others, could not
consider practicable.   Colonel Toll suggested some
alterations in the movements for the following day,
which in themselves promised well, but might
easily lead to confusion, because time was wanting
to arrange them with certainty.   To the Author
the affair appeared less bad than had been supposed,
even in the case that the circumstances had all been
correctly reported; he, however, also considered
the whole intelligence as very doubtful, and was of
opinion that things should be allowed to take their
course, and no new measures be adopted.   It is
usual, in a council of war, that he who advises
doing nothing carries his point, and this was no
exception.   Colonel Toll adopted the Author's
view, and it was determined to advise the Emperor
accordingly.   The Emperor opened the door;
General Phull and Colonel Toll were admitted,
and the conference came to an end.   On the following day, it appeared that the news had been false.
The camp of Drissa was reached without the dis-

covery of any enemy on the road, other than such
as was pressing the rear guard.

This transaction thoroughly satisfied the Author
that such a management of the army could not
come to good. It is probable that the Emperor's
confidence in Phull received a new shock; for the
latter was no more sent for by him, as was constantly happening earlier.

The Author now endeavoured to direct the
observation of General Phull himself to the loss of
the Emperor's confidence, and the other disadvantages of his position, and to excite in him the
thought of a retreat from it. He told him, without
reserve, that although he doubted the capability of
General Barclay to direct a large army with success against Buonaparte, yet that he seemed to him
a calm and determined man, and a thorough
soldier; that the favour of the Emperor was visibly
inclining more and more towards him; and that
if General Phull could persuade the Emperor to
make over to him the chief command, at least
unity of action and coherence of movements would
be the result. The Author was secure of the noble
feeling he would have to encounter; for the general,
however confined in his views, and lost in his own
ideas, had no trace of egotism in his composition.

On July 8., when the head-quarters of the
Emperor was entering the camp of Drissa, he sent
for General Phull, in order, with him and other
officers of his suite, to ride through the lines.
Phull explained, in detail, the objects of the works,

in the course of which various minor difficulties
here and there suggested themselves. The Emperor appeared as if looking to his officers for
corroboration of General Phull's remarks.   He
was, however, surrounded by doubtful countenances.   The Colonel Michaud, aide-de-camp to
the Emperor, who had from the Sardinian service
entered that of Russia, and had served in the
Sardinian engineer corps, was a man of professional
authority, and passed for one of instruction and
capacity.   He appeared less than any one satisfied
with the whole matter; and it was he who finally
declared himself aloud against the camp of Drissa,
and decided the determination of the Emperor.

At first, indeed, it seemed as if the idea was not
to be abandoned; for the Author was sent the following day to inspect the ground on the other side
of the river, in order to judge in what position it
would be possible to meet the enemy, if he should
cross the river in order to outflank the Russian
front.

Meanwhile the events of the war had taken a
shape by no means in consonance with the plans of
General Phull.   When the moment arrived for
forwarding to General Bagration the order for an
offensive movement on the French rear, the Russian
courage failed; and either the representations of
that general, or the sensation of weakness, brought
it to this — that Bagration took a line of retreat, with
a view to a later junction with the 1st army of the
West; a resolution by which was avoided a leading

calamity incident to the plan of Phull, viz. the total destruction of this second army.

The Emperor, therefore, saw his plan of campaign, on which he had at first depended, half destroyed; he saw his army at Drissa about one sixth weaker than he had expected; he heard from all sides significant expressions of opinion respecting the camp; he had lost his confidence in the plan and its author; he felt the difficulty of commanding such an army. General Barclay made the most urgent remonstrances against a battle at Drissa, and demanded, as a preliminary, the junction of the two armies; in which he was perfectly right. Under these circumstances the Emperor took the resolution of giving up the command; of placing General Barclay, for the moment, at the head of the whole army; and of proceeding in person to Moscow, and thence to St. Petersburg, in order every where to push forward the reinforcements of the army, to provide for its subsistence and other wants, and to set on foot a militia which would place under arms a great portion of the nation. The Emperor could not take a better resolution.

General Phull felt himself in a very constrained position. For several days the Emperor had not spoken with him, and the court followers began entirely to avoid him. The Author now pressed him to anticipate the breach; to go himself to the Emperor, and advise him to give up the command unconditionally to Barclay. Not without a pang did the general determine upon this step, which did his heart the more honour. He went from the spot to the Emperor. The Emperor received him kindly, and appeared in his resolve only to follow the advice of the general, which, however, could hardly have been the fact; for, had it been so, he would not have thus decided without opposition and discussion.

As it had now been determined not to give battle in the Drissa camp, and it was also impossible to effect there a junction with Bagration, it was proposed by Prince Alexander of Wirtemberg, uncle to the Emperor, a general of cavalry, and present at head-quarters in his capacity of governor of Witebsk, to occupy a strong position near that town which he had in his eye, and described as impregnable. It was thus determined to march upon Witebsk.

The French had not yet passed by the position of Drissa. The road to Witebsk by Polozk was still open; and as the enemy had not yet pressed on strongly, it might be hoped, under the protection of the Dwina, to execute this march in safety, although from the position of Witebsk it was, in fact, a flank march. It was hoped that, in any case, a junction might be effected with Bagration in Witebsk. At all events it was the road to Smolensko, at which place it falls into the great road to Moscow, and affords a natural line of retreat, as well for a junction with Bagration as with the reinforcements on their march from the interior. These were reasons which weighed far more with General Barclay than the representations of Prince

Alexander of Wirtemburg of the strength of the position of Witebsk. The Author felt himself relieved, and rejoiced when he saw affairs taking the turn of a retreat in this direction.

In truth, the condition of the Russian army was still one of great anxiety, and the state of military affairs in general any thing but favourable; but the mind of man is so constituted, that he considers his relief from the nearest and most pressing of many evils a positive blessing, and indulges the most cheerful expectations on the slightest appearance of improvement.

The Emperor had thus resolved to leave the army. He ordered, however, his head-quarters to remain with it, partly to avoid too much observation, and perhaps the excitement of a questionable spirit in the troops if he should appear definitively to abandon them; partly because he could not foresee the possible turn of events, and wished to preserve to himself the option of a return. He privately put it to the choice of General Phull, whether he would remain at head-quarters, or betake himself to St. Petersburg. General Phull chose, as a soldier naturally would choose, the first alternative. So long as several persons of his rank remained, he thought that course not beneath his dignity. General Barclay, however, to whom this crowd and this number of officers of rank were very unacceptable at head-quarters, made arrangements that the Imperial head-quarters should always be a day's march in advance of the army; by which it came under the category of the heavy baggage, which was very galling to the officers attached to it. By degrees the Emperor called away the principal officers, one after another, to special duties; and General Phull felt that he could not with propriety remain longer in such a position, and departed for St. Petersburg.

The head-quarters of General Barclay had undergone an alteration in the persons of the general of the staff and the quartermaster-general. General Labanow had obtained the command of the guards under the Grand Duke Constantine, which formed the 6th corps. Lieutenant-General the Marquis Paulucci had succeeded to the post of General Labanow. This officer had distinguished himself in the wars against the Turks and Persians. He was a restless genius, with a strange faculty of persuasion. Heaven knows how they had come to the conclusion that, with such qualities and abilities as he possessed, he was specially fitted for the great movements and emergencies of war. He united, however, with much wrong-headedness a good deal of ill nature; and it was soon evident that no man could do well with him, and his appointment lasted but a few days. He was called away to St. Petersburg, and a little later appointed governor of Riga, to replace General Essen in the defence of that important place. He was himself replaced, on General Barclay's staff, by Lieutenant-General Yermalof, who had served earlier in the artillery.

This was a man some forty years old, of an ambitious, ardent, and strong character, and not without understanding and cultivation. He was, to all intents, preferable to any one hitherto employed; for it was at least to be expected from him that he would ensure obedience every where to the orders of the Chief, and introduce a certain energy into measures in general, which would be felt as a kind of essential compliment to the somewhat soft and inactive mode of proceeding and habits of the general commanding. As, however, he had not much reflected previously on the greater movements and measures of a war, nor arrived at clear perceptions in his own mind on such a subject, he felt, when the moment arrived for decision and action, how strange it was to him. He therefore confined himself to the general business of the army, and left to the quartermaster-general the details of tactics and strategy in the field.

The quartermaster-general's office was originally held, as we have seen, by General Muchin, a Russian to the bone, who, understanding no foreign language, had necessarily read none but Russian books. He had been appointed to this post solely for the having distinguished himself in the making of maps and surveys, a branch which, in an army comparatively behind-hand in instruction, is commonly received as the representative of all military science. The deficiencies of such an appointment of necessity soon became obvious. He was replaced by Lieutenant-Colonel Toll.

Colonel Toll was a man some thirty years of age,

conspicuous for instruction among the officers on the staff. He was a character of tolerable parts and decided will. Having long busied himself with the study of the *grande guerre*, and well acquainted with the works of the most recent writers, he was immersed in those of the most recent of all, Jomini. He was therefore in some measure equal to the circumstances; and though far from that assurance of his case which is founded on one's own reflection, nor endowed with that creative genius which could conceive a comprehensive and coherent plan, he was adequate both in capacity and knowledge to the immediate exigencies of the moment, and capable of preventing courses altogether antiquated and unsuited to the time and circumstances.

He was but half in possession of General Barclay's confidence; partly because that officer was of a cold temperament, which did not lightly coalesce with that of another; partly because Colonel Toll himself was entirely deficient in a certain observance, a delicate tact of conduct which is absolutely necessary in such situations: he was distinguished for his roughness towards both superiors and inferiors.

Colonel Wolzogen had remained at the headquarters of General Barclay. This officer by his distinguished acquirements, which probably far outweighed any at that time existing in the Russian army, and a mind rich in resources, would have been signally qualified for the post of quarter-

master-general, if a certain staff-officer kind of
pedantry had not at times diverted him from the
use of his own strong natural powers of reflection,
and made him less fit for that office. The man
who means to move in such a medium as the element of war, should bring with him nothing from
books but the general education of his understanding. If he extracts from them, on the contrary,
ideas cut and dried, not derived from the impulse
of the moment, the stream of events will dash his
structure to the ground before it is finished. He
will never be intelligible to others, men of natural
genius; and least of all in the most distinguished
among them, those who know their own wishes
and intentions, will he inspire confidence. Thus
it was with Colonel Wolzogen. He was, moreover,
too imperfectly acquainted with the Russian language not continually to remind the Russians that
he was a foreigner. A great propensity to politics
was in his character. He was too clever to believe,
that as a stranger, with foreign notions, he could
win confidence enough and authority enough over
the mass of the army to present his ideas openly
and without reserve; he did, however, believe that
the generality of mankind was so feeble and incon-
sistent that an able and consistent man might, with
a little dexterity, lead them whither he would.
This notion produced something of concealment in
his demeanour and proceedings, which the Russians
in general construed into a spirit of intrigue. This
was enough to make him an object of their sus-

picion; and they did not ask themselves what his objects could be, or whether, under the circumstances, they could be other than the good of the army and the cause in which we were all embarked. The man who aims at leading others without their perceiving it should have insinuating peculiarities. Such had not fallen to the lot of Wolzogen: his manner was dry and grave, and hence he failed in acquiring for his talents a sphere of activity proportioned to their merit. He was from these causes passed over in the appointment to the quartermaster-generalship; but resolved to make the campaign in the suite of Barclay, in the hope of being of occasional utility. How far this hope was justified, or whether he occasionally prevented pernicious measures, I cannot pronounce. To this, however, his influence must have been restricted; for, from this period to Barclay's change of command, very little took place which emanated from the positive will of the Russian leaders. Wolzogen was daily an object of increased suspicion to the Russians, though Barclay in public exhibited no great confidence in him. They looked upon him, however, with a kind of superstitious aversion, as an evil spirit who brought misfortune upon the measures of their chief.

The Author had profited by the presence of Count Lieven at the camp of Drissa to obtain, through his intervention, an appointment on the general staff.* General Lieven and Colonel Wal-

* He had wished to have been attached to the rear-guard.

zogen negotiated this with General Barclay, who gave the order for it on the march to Polozk, without having spoken to General Yermalof or Colonel Toll on the subject: these two took this very ill, as well as the appointment which followed in like manner of Lieutenant-Colonel von Lutzow to the 5th corps; and this occasioned an unpleasant scene directed against Colonel Wolzogen. The appointments meanwhile remained undisturbed.*

By these means the Author came to be attached to General Count Peter Pahlen, who commanded the rear-guard which was to cover the retreat along the right bank of the Dwina.

General Count Pahlen was esteemed one of the best cavalry officers of the Russian army. He was a man not quite 40 years of age, simple in his habits, open in his character; not, indeed, endowed with great intellectual powers or scientific acquirements, but of a lively understanding and talents for society. As a soldier he had served with dis-

---

* Leo von Lutzow, younger brother of the famous leader of the free corps, served before the year 1806 in the Prussian foot-guards: in 1809 he entered the Austrian service, and on the peace of 1810 he went to Spain: made prisoner in 1811 on the surrender of Valencia, he escaped in the south of France: he made his way on foot through Switzerland and South Germany, and afterwards through North Germany, Poland, and Russia, passing through the middle of the French army, till he joined the Russian, which he reached at Drissa, and was attached as lieutenant-colonel to the general staff. The Author is not acquainted with another instance of a German officer who had served against France in all these three wars, the Austrian, the Spanish, and the Russian.

tinction; was very brave, calm, and determined, qualities which in his position must rank among the first. As he spoke German perfectly, and his habits were rather German than Russian, an appointment under him was doubly agreeable to the Author. It was, however, an unpleasant surprise to the latter to find himself attached to the corps as first officer of the general staff, first quartermaster. The Author's express wish had been to be made either second officer or aide-de-camp, being, as he was, as good as ignorant of the Russian language. The fact was, that Colonel Toll saw with satisfaction any thing which stamped an appointment, effected by Colonel Wolzogen, from the beginning with unfitness.

Count Pahlen received the Author with a kind of stately indifference, and asked immediately whether he knew Russian; to which he was of course obliged to reply in the negative, for a month's study at Wilna had hardly advanced him as far as a pair of the most necessary phrases. The Author proposed to Count Pahlen to consider, and employ him rather as his aide-de-camp than as chief of his staff, which, however, Count Pahlen declined: the Author thus found himself at once in a false position, and nothing remained for him but the determination to gain the respect of the Russians by avoiding neither fatigue nor danger.

CHAPTER II.

GENERAL REVIEW OF THE INCIDENTS OF THE CAM-
PAIGN OF 1812 IN RUSSIA.

THE campaign falls naturally into two divisions;
that which preceded the retreat of the French, and
that retreat.

PART I.

The war is carried on on five separate theatres.
Two to the left of the road from Wilna to Moscow
are occupied by the left wing; two to the right of
it by the right wing; and the huge mass of the
centre makes the fifth.

1. On the lower Dwina, Macdonald with 30,000
men observes the garrison of Riga, which is 10,000
strong: the latter, indeed, was increased in September by 12,000 men under Steinheil from Finland; but they did not remain, and were joined to
the army of Wittgenstein.

2. On the middle Dwina towards Polozk, Oudinot
is placed in the first instance with 40,000 men,
afterwards Oudinot and St. Cyr together, with
65,000, against Wittgenstein, who at first had
30,000, and finally was increased to 50,000.

3. In south Lithuania, facing the morasses of
Precipiez, Schwarzenberg and Reynier, 51,000
strong, against Tormasow, who musters 35,000, and

is joined afterwards by Tschitschagow with the army
of the Moldau, 35,000 strong.

4. General Dombrowski with his division and
some cavalry, about 10,000 strong, observes Bobruisk and the General Hertel, who with 12,000
men forms a reserve corps near Mozyr.

5. Finally, in the middle space is the main force
of France, 300,000 men, opposed to the two main
armies of Russia under Barclay and Bagration,
120,000 men strong, and destined for the conquest
of Moscow.

The numbers here given are those of the various
corps at the period of their crossing the Niemen:
these, however, soon melted down, so that Oudinot
and St. Cyr together never really mustered 65,000
men, nor Schwarzenberg and Reynier 51,000.
The transition from the first distribution of these
five main bodies, which occupied the month of July,
is alone somewhat involved. From this period all
is simplified. The centre creeps on towards Moscow; on the flanks the struggle proceeds with
dubious results till the period, the middle of October, when Buonaparte with the centre is obliged to
retrace his steps, and at the same time the invaders
on either flank begin to show weakness, and either
to open out eccentrically like Schwarzenberg, or to
allow themselves to be pressed back on the road of
the centre like Oudinot and St. Cyr.

The Russian army on the frontier, at the opening
of the campaign, was disposed in three main bodies.

1. The 1st army of the West under Barclay,

90,000 strong, stood with its right wing (Wittgenstein) on the Baltic; its left (Doctorof) towards Grodno; the head-quarters in Wilna.

2. The 2d army of the West under Bagration, 45,000 strong, extended from Grodno to Muchawetz; head-quarters at Wolkowisk.

3. The reserve army, so called, under Tormasow, beyond the marshes in south Volhynia, 35,000; head-quarters in Luzk.

4. To the above are to be added 10,000 Cossacks, chiefly under Platoff, with Bagration. Total in 1st line 180,000 men.

In 2d line were the reserve divisions, formed of 3d battalions and 5th squadrons, along the Dwina and Dnieper, 35,000 men; employed as reinforcements to Wittgenstein, as garrisons to Riga and Bobruisk, and as part of General Hertel's corps, and therefore came into activity somewhat later.

The French, with their allies, advanced in four main bodies.

1. The left wing, Macdonald, 10th corps, 30,000 men, crossed the Niemen at Tilsit; destination against Riga.

2. The centre; Buonaparte in person:

1st corps	-	-	-	Davoust	-	⁀ 72,000 men.
2d	-	-	-	-	Oudinot -	- 37,000
3d	-	-	-	-	Ney -	- 39,000
4th	-	-	-	-	Eugene	- 45,000
5th	-	-	-	-	St. Cyr	- 25,000
The guards		-	-	Mortier	-	- 47,000
Three cavalry reserve corps, Murat					-	- 32,000
						297,000

This mass crossed the Niemen at two points; 230,000 men at Kowno, and 67,000 at Pilona, three miles above Kowno; and was destined against Barclay.

3. Attached also to the centre, under Jerome:

5th corps	-	Poniatowski	-	-	- 36,000 men.
7th	-	- Reynier -	-	-	- 17,000
8th	-	- Vandamme	-	-	- 17,000
Cavalry corps	Latour Maubourg		-	-	8,000
					78,000

This army crossed near Grodno, and was directed against Bagration.

4. The right wing, under Schwarzenberg, crossed the Bug near Drohyczyn, and appeared to be directed against Tormasow.—Total 439,000.

Buonaparte's plan was to cross at Kowno on the 24th June with 230,000 men, and to drive back Barclay as quickly as possible. The 78,000 men under Jerome were to cross a week later, on the 1st of July, and to march against Bagration: by this delay he hoped to induce both Bagration, and Barclay's left wing under Doctorof, to postpone their retreat, and then to cut them off entirely from Barclay by detaching troops against them from the centre. The 67,000 men under Eugene, who were also to cross later, i.e. on the 30th June, were intended to cover the right flank of the main army of the centre, and to form an army of communication with Jerome. Schwarzenberg and Macdonald were to advance towards their object of operation, regulating their progress by that of the centre.

The advance of the French, i.e. the campaign up to the period of abandoning Moscow, falls again into two divisions.

The first comprehends the movements of the French, having for their object the separation and cutting off of the Russians, and the Russian march for the junction of their forces. These movements terminate at the beginning of August in the neighbourhood of Witebsk and Orsza for the French, and for the Russians at Smolensko.

The second division includes, simply, the entire advance to Moscow.

In either division there occur two periods. ' In the first, because the French twice made distinct halts; the first at Wilna, the second at Witebsk. In the second, because the French offensive ceases with the occupation of Moscow, and their sojourn there assumes the character of the defensive. We shall therefore have four periods previous to the retreat.

FIRST PERIOD. *Advance of the French, up to their first halt at Wilna—about three weeks, from June* 24. *to the middle of July.*

The passage of the Niemen was thus conducted:— Napoleon, on the 24th and 25th, crossed with his enormous masses by three bridges, but at one point, and reached Wilna the 29th. Immediately after the passage he detached Oudinot, strengthened with one cavalry division, to the left against Wittgenstein, who, at the moment, was posted near

Keidany, in order, if possible, to separate him from Barclay. He made Ney follow, partly to support Oudinot, partly in order to become more securely master of the right bank of the Wilia.

Wittgenstein in fact met with Oudinot's advanced guard at Wilkomir, but reached the main army when abreast of Swanziany, in which direction both the French corps followed him. From Wilna Buonaparte sent some 50,000 men under Davoust by Ozmiana, Woloschin, and Rakow, upon Minsk, to effect the contemplated separation of Bagration from Barclay. There remained then some 110,000 men under his immediate command, who, partly under Murat, followed Barclay by Swanziany, partly (the guards) remained at Wilna.

Barclay, with the centre of the 1st army of the West, had commenced his retreat from Wilna the 26th of June by Swanziany towards Drissa; but so slowly, that on July 2. he was still at Swanziany, and both Wittgenstein and Doctorof were able to join him. The latter had broken up from Lida on the 27th, and had taken the direction of Ozmiana. Here he fell upon an advanced corps of Davoust, and made a forced march on Swir, which he reached on the 1st of July, narrowly missing a detachment of the cavalry of the guard sent against him from Wilna. On the 2d he successfully effected his junction with Barclay at Swanziany. Barclay reached the camp at Drissa on the 10th of July.

On the 30th of June, Eugene crossed at Pilona, and directed his march on Novi Trochi and

Anuszyski. Buonaparte, however, withdrew from this mass the 6th corps back to Wilna.

Eugene persevered in his movement as far as Dewinicki, which he reached on the 10th of July. As, however, at this time Davoust was already in Minsk, and Bagration had gone in a due south direction by Bobruisk, Eugene was obliged to quit his direction, and take a new one by Smorgoni, Wilienka, and Kamenje, upon Witebsk; by which also this great mass again united itself with the main army.

On the 1st July, Jerome advanced by Grodno and Byalystock towards Novogrodeck.

Bagration had broken up from Wolkowisk on the 29th June, and marched by Slonim and Novogrodeck to Nikolajef, where, on the 4th July, he wished to pass the Niemen. When he ascertained the presence of Davoust in Woloschin, he turned towards Mir, in order to march by Schwerschin upon Minsk; as, however, he touched in Schwerschin upon an advanced corps of Davoust, he took only a cavalry detachment belonging to Doctorof's corps, under General Dorochof, and went to Njeswich, in order, by Sluzk, Bobruisk, and Mohilew, to reach Barclay's army. He remained three days from the 10th July in Njeswich, in order to collect his troops, and give time to the baggage and artillery to gain the advance.

Tormasow was still in Volhynia, and had his head-quarters in Lutzk, where he assembled his army.

On July 10. the distribution of the army was as follows:—

THE FRENCH.

Macdonald, with 30,000 men, between Rossiena and Schwalja.
Oudinot, 40,000, Solock.
Ney, 39,000, Rimsziani.
Murat, 51,000, Widzy.
Buonaparte, guards, St. Cyr, 72,000, Wilna.
Davoust, 50,000, Minsk.
Eugene, 40,000, Dipnischki.
Jerome, 5th and 8th corps and the cavalry, 61,000, Nowo-grodeck.
Reynier, 17,000, between Wolkowisk and Nowogrodeck.
Schwarzenberg, 34,000, Pruschany.

THE RUSSIANS.

Barclay, 100,000, Camp of Drissa.
Bagration, 45,000, Njeswich.
Tormasow, 35,000, Lutzk.

It was about this time that the French army entered on a formal suspension of operations. Buonaparte, with the flower of his army, remained a fortnight quiet at Wilna. (He individually left Wilna on the 16th July.) Murat, Ney, and Oudinot pressed the Russians so feebly, that the latter were able to spend fifteen days on the march of thirty miles from Wilna to Drissa, and then to remain some eight days longer before the latter. Even Davoust halted in Minsk four days before moving on Mohilew. Eugene continued his flank movement on Witebsk, which, however, fell within the circle of the space already embraced.

This suspension was produced by the great difficulties of subsistence; the enormous multitude of stragglers, as well as of sick, produced by a violent and cold rain, which fell for eight days together towards the end of June.

SECOND PERIOD. *From the end of the first halt to the second inclusive —from middle of July to August 8., three weeks.*

Towards the middle of July, Buonaparte set his force in motion towards Glubocköe, moving thitherward himself on the 16th. While he was meditating thence the attack, or rather the surrounding of the Drissa camp, with his whole central army exclusive of Davoust, Jerome, and Eugene, Barclay gave up the idea of fighting a battle in the camp, and determined upon a further retreat upon the Moscow road, and thus in the direction of Witebsk in the first instance. He broke up on the 16th, took his way along the right bank of the Dwina by Polozk, and reached Witebsk the 23d. He left Wittgenstein behind with 25,000 men in the neighbourhood of Polozk, to cover the roads to Petersburgh.

Buonaparte despatched Oudinot with his corps and a cavalry division after Wittgenstein, and followed Barclay with the rest towards Witebsk, which he approached on the 26th.

Bagration broke up on the 13th from Njeswisch, marched by Sluzk, Glusk, and Bobruisk over the Beresina, and then upon Staroi-Bychow on the Dnieper, which he reached on the 21st. He proceeded up the stream towards Mohilew, in order to avail himself of the bridges there.

Davoust had been obliged to send from Minsk 6000 cavalry to the main army at Orsza. After making several other detachments he marched with his main body on Mohilew, which he reached on the 20th July. He had now but 20,000 men remaining, with whom he put himself in motion against Bagration, who had 45,000. He found, about a mile and a half from Mohilew, a strong position at the village of Saltanowka, in which he waited for Bagration on the 22d, and was attacked by him ineffectually on the 23d. The latter had not the courage to devote his whole force to this attack, nor time to turn the position. It therefore remained rather a feint on his part with his cavalry and the corps of Rajefskoi, while he was throwing a bridge over the river at Staroi-Bychow. He effected his passage the 24th, and retired by Mstislaw upon Smolensko, which he reached on the 4th August, two days after Bagration.

The mass of troops united under Jerome, which was immediately destined against Bagration, and by the 10th July had advanced to Novogrodeck, followed Bagration's march to Mir. There Platoff laid an ambuscade for his advanced guard, which occasioned it severe loss, and which seems to have made Jerome cautious. He allowed at least Bagration to delay for three days in Njeswisch, and was still there himself on the 16th, when Buonaparte sent him severe remonstrances on his slowness, and ordered him to place himself under orders of Davoust. Discontented with this, he forthwith left the army. His corps d'armée was broken up as follows.

The 8th corps (Westphalian), the command of which had been taken from Vandamme, and made over pro tempore to Tharreau, marched by Minsk to Orsza, and thus joined the grand army. Ponia-towski with the 5th corps followed Bagration only to Romanowa, where commenced the great forests, and retired thence by Igumen to Mohilew, which he reached six days after the action there. Latour Maubourg followed Bagration as far as Glusk, but could only reach that place on the 24th. As he could not proceed by Bobruisk, which is a fortress, he crossed the Beresina by Beresino, and so on to Mohilew, where he arrived only on the 5th August.

Reynier with the 7th corps received orders to move against Tormasow. Buonaparte had it in view, against the sense indeed of his treaty with Austria, to draw Schwarzenberg to the grand army, and to entrust Reynier with the defence of Muchawetz and Precipiez, for which he considered him sufficient, not valuing Tormasow at higher than 10,000 men. Reynier, therefore, was ordered back upon Slonim, and thence towards Muchawetz.

Schwarzenberg had occupied Muchawetz and Pina from Pruschany with a chain of outposts towards Volhynia, which extended 25 miles from Brezesck-Litewski to Pinsk. Reynier thought pro-

per to dissolve this. He found himself on the 25th
July at Chomsk, while the brigade of Klengel
was at Kobrin, and some smaller detachments at
Pinsk and Brezesck-Litewski.

Tormasow, in the middle of July, received orders
to press forward on the rear of the French. He
moved on the 17th, and advanced on a very extended line; for while his main force was moving
by Ratno on Kobrin, his flank detachments extended to Brezesck-Litewski and Pinsk. This made
Reynier uncertain as to the direction of his march;
and it thus happened that Tormasow had time to
advance with his main body on the brigade of
Klengel, while his detached corps arriving from
Brezesck-Litewski completely turned the enemy,
and forced him, after an obstinate action, to lay
down his arms, which occasioned a loss to General
Reynier of 6000 men. Reynier hastened to
Klengel's support; but only reached Antopol, and
found himself compelled to retire thence towards
Slonim. Schwarzenberg, better informed of the
strength of Tormasow, had not obeyed the order of
Napoleon, but had remained at Slonim, whence he
now moved forward to receive Reynier. With the
consent of Buonaparte, subsequently obtained, he
remained exclusively on this theatre of operations.

Macdonald had moved forward the Prussians
under General Grawert towards Riga, who on the
19th of July fell upon General Lewis with part of
the garrison of Riga, and drove him back, after a
lively action, on Dahlenkirchen. Macdonald him-

self had gone with Grandjean's division to Jacobstadt, where he remained for some weeks.

On the 24th of July, then, the distribution of
either army was as follows:—

Macdonald, 20,000, before Riga, and 10,000 in Jacobstadt.
Oudinot, 40,000, against Wittgenstein, who, with 30,000, is at
    Polozk.
Buonaparte, 180,000, against Barclay, who has 75,000 near
    Witebsk.
St. Cyr, 25,000, a kind of reserve, near Uszacz.
Davoust, 50,000, against Bagration, near Mohilew.
Bagration, 45,000, between Mohilew and Mstislaw.
Poniatowski, 44,000, between Beresino and Mohilew.
The 8th corps, 17,000, near Borissow.
Schwarzenberg, 34,000, near Slonim.
Reynier, 17,000, near Chomsk, against Tormasow, 35,000, near
    Kobrin.

If both in this statement and the former we
have given the numbers as they originally stood, it
is only for the better comprehension of the original
distribution of the forces. We may otherwise
assume that by about the 26th July they had
lost, on the French side, at least one fourth by
stragglers, sick, and casualties in battle. The
Russian loss was less, since their retrograde march
on their own soil could be better provided for, and
facilitated by magazines.

The French were also weakened by detachments,
but Davoust principally; the others less so than
might be imagined, as they formed stragglers into
battalions, and used them for the occupation of posts.

Barclay had pushed out a strong rear-guard
from Witebsk against the French, on the left bank

of the Dwina, which, on the road to Beszenkowicki, between Ostrowno and Witebsk, had continual and lively actions with Murat: on the 25th under General Tolstoy Ostermann; the 26th under General Konownitzin; the 27th under General Pahlen, which lasted up to the neighbourhood of Witebsk.

On the 27th, Buonaparte reckoned on coming to blows with Barclay; but the latter had only delayed four days at Witebsk, and on receiving accounts that Bagration had taken his way to Smolensko, had marched on the 27th in two columns on the roads of Rudnia and Poreczie to join Bagration. Barclay reached Smolensko the 2d of August, Bagration the 4th, where they found a reinforcement of 8000 men. The two armies might now amount to 120,000 men, exclusive of Cossacks.

Barclay took the chief command; but not with entire authority, as Bagration had only accepted of his own will a subordinate position. The armies remained distinct.

Buonaparte sat down at Witebsk, and distributed his corps between the Dwina and Dnieper.

Here ensued the second halt of the French army, which lasted to the 8th August. Before it terminated, the corps of Jerome, Eugene, and Davoust, which had been detached against Bagration, rejoined the main army : Eugene on the 24th at Briszikowa on the Ula ; Davoust on the 21st at Dubrowna on the Dnieper ; the 8th corps on the 4th August at Orsza, where Junot took its command. Poniatowski with the 5th corps remained till the 8th at Mohilew, whence he despatched Latour Maubourg with the 4th cavalry corps and the division Dombrowski against Bobruisk and General Hertel. Latour Maubourg returned ultimately also to the great army; but Dombrowski remained in that quarter, to cover Minsk, till the period of the retreat. Poniatowski joined the centre at the moment of its advance on Smolensko. Reynier, as we have mentioned, had been sent to Volhynia.

During this period of the quiescence and reformation of the centre, Wittgenstein had retired a day's march from the Dwina on the road of Druja towards Sebesch and Petersburg; and in danger of being attacked on one hand by Oudinot, who was advancing from Polozk on the road to Sebesch, on the other by Macdonald, who was arrived at Jacobstadt, had resolved to attack Oudinot before Macdonald was enough advanced to co-operate with the latter. He advanced, therefore, from Razizi by Kochanowo against Kliastizi, and fell upon Oudinot the 31st July with 20,000 men near Jacubowo, and beat him. On the pursuit, however, the following day, his advanced guard under General Kulniew, after crossing the Drissa, suffered such a defeat as would have overbalanced the advantage of the day before, if General Verdier had not in his turn stumbled on the main body of Wittgenstein, and been compelled to retire with great loss, by which the ultimate advantage remained on the side of Russia, inasmuch as Oudinot gave up further advance, and was obliged to reinforce himself from the corps of St. Cyr. Wittgenstein followed as far as Polozk; and not feeling himself strong enough to attack this place, considered it better to resume his position between Druja and Drissa. Schwarzenberg was advancing against Tormasow.

Such was the state of things to the 8th of August, and perhaps this suspension would have lasted somewhat longer if Barclay had not made an attempt at the offensive.

The campaign had now lasted six weeks. The line on which the French had advanced amounted to fifty miles from the frontier, its extent from the Baltic to Muchawetz by Witebsk and Orza to about 150.

The French had suffered considerably from privation and toil, and occasionally from fighting. It is to be added that they had detached considerable bodies, and we may conjecture that the original superiority of the centre over Barclay was much diminished. In fact the force under Buonaparte, according to the lists of the day, on the 3d of August, was not above 185,000 men.

Of the 375,000 men originally forming the centre, keeping to original numbers, some 90,000 had been detached under Oudinot, St. Cyr, Latour Maubourg, and Reynier; 285,000 ought therefore to have remained. The 100,000 deficient from this number were, for the most part, clear loss; for the French had scarcely made any smaller detachments, such as garrisons and the like. Their loss, therefore, up to this time reached to a fourth of their original strength. Schwarzenberg and Oudinot had suffered in somewhat similar proportion; for the first, together with Reynier, had only 42,000 of their original 51,000, and Oudinot and St. Cyr had only 35,000 out of 65,000. Macdonald had suffered less.

The distribution of the 185,000 under Buonaparte was as follows:—

Murat and Ney at Rudnia.

The three divisions of the 1st corps not with Davoust at Babinowicki.

The guard at Witebsk.

Eugene at Surasch and Welisch.

Davoust and Junot on the left bank of the Dnieper.

THIRD PERIOD. *From the attempt at the offensive of the Russian main army to the loss of Moscow —from the 8th August to the 15th September, five weeks.*

The distribution of the French army, for the most part in cantonments, was at least extended enough to afford hope of advantage from a rapid offensive to the extent of placing isolated corps in difficulty. Even though no general defeat of it should result, it might prove a brilliant feat of arms to Russia, calculated to exalt her moral strength, and to debilitate her enemy, both physically and morally, on which every thing depended for the success of Russia.

Barclay, therefore, resolved leaving behind only the division of Newerofskoi, which had been advanced to Krasnoi, to direct both armies on Rudnia, as the central point of the enemy's position; and commenced his march for this purpose, on this and the neighbouring roads, in three columns, on the 8th of August. The result of this unsuspected movement was, that Platoff fell, with the Russian advanced guard, on that of the French under Sebastiani at Inkowo, and drove it in with great loss. But Barclay on the first day conceived the apprehension that the main body of the enemy was on the Poreczie road, and that he was on the point of making a blow in the air. He became anxious about his retreat, gave up the offensive, and took up a position on the Poreczie road.

By this uncompleted attack the French were roused, and Buonaparte resolved to resume his own offensive operations. On the 14th, all the corps hitherto on the right bank of the Dnieper crossed it at Rasasna, and advanced on Smolensko; while Barclay, who at the end of three days recognised his mistake, wished to make a new attempt on the Rudnia road. The French movement, however, called him back on the 16th from the neighbourhood of Kasplia to Smolensko.

On the 15th, the Russian division Newerofskoi, which remained still near Krasnoi, was attacked by Murat, and driven back with great loss. On the

16th, the French attacked Smolensko, into which
Bagration had in haste thrown the corps of Rajefskoi.   On the 17th, this corps was relieved by one
from the 1st army under Doctorof, and Bagration
took with the 2d army a position further back,
behind the Kolodnia, on the Moscow road.   The
French continued their attack on the suburbs of
Smolensko, and became masters of them towards
evening.   In the night of the 18th, the Russians
abandoned Smolensko; but remained on the 18th
on the right bank of the Dnieper, opposite the
place, and prevented the passage of the French.
In the night of the 19th, Barclay began his retreat
with the 1st army; and, in fact, as the Moscow road
runs for some leagues parallel with the river, and near
it, at first in the direction of Poreczie, and then by
a side road towards Lubino, two miles from Smolensko, again into the Moscow road.   This gave
occasion to the affair of the rear-guard at Valutina
Gora, in which about one third of the respective
armies were engaged.   The strength of the Russian
position, which lay behind marshy hollows, enabled
them to maintain the field of battle till dark, and to
secure their retreat.

The affairs of Smolensko and Valutina Gora
cost the French 20,000 men, and the Russians
about as many.

From Valutina Gora to Borodino affairs of
rear-guard were of daily occurrence, but none of
great importance.   It usually happened that 10,000
or 15,000 cavalry, supported by some 10,000

infantry, were opposed to a similar force on some point, and kept each other in check.

On August 27th, the Russian army was joined by 15,000 men under Miloradowitsch.

On the 29th Kutusow arrived, and received the command from Barclay, who remained at the head of the 1st army of the West. Benningsen was chief of the general staff.

On the 4th of September the Russian army had reached Borodino, where it was reinforced by 10,000 militia; on the 5th occurred the affair of the advanced posts of the left wing; on the 6th both sides reposed; on the 7th occurred the battle, in which the Russians were about 120,000, the French about 130,000. After a loss of some 30,000 on the Russian side, and 20,000 on the French, Kutusow, early on the 8th, continued his retreat on Moscow. Buonaparte pursued with the army, leaving at Mojaisk Junot's corps, now reduced to a few thousands.

The retreat of the Russians was attended by constant, but generally unimportant, affairs of rear-guard. It was only on the 10th of September that the strength of a position at Krimskoie gave Miloradowitsch opportunity for a strong resistance, which cost the French 2000 men.

On September 14th the Russian army passed through Moscow, and the French entered it; at the end of a march of 50 miles from Smolensko, performed in 27 days.

The Russians, on the 14th, executed a trifling

march on the road of Riazan, which was covered
on the right by the course of the Moskwa. They
were quiet on the 15th; on the 16th made again a
short march on that road as far as the passage of
the Moskwa, four miles from the town; and then
on the 17th and 18th turned in two side marches
to behind the Pachra to Podolsk; there they remained the 19th, and on the 20th made another
side march to Krasnoi Pachra, on the old road of
Kaluga, where they remained till the 26th.

During this 3d period Wittgenstein had determined on an attempt against the division of Grandjean, of Macdonald's corps, posted at Dunaburg,
when he received accounts that Oudinot, strengthened by St. Cyr, was advancing against him. Although he had drawn to himself the garrison of
Dunaburg, the fortifications of that place not being
ready, he was yet scarce 20,000 strong. He resolved,
notwithstanding, to march against Oudinot. On
the 16th August he arrived before Polozk, and
found Oudinot posted with his rear towards that
town. He attacked him on the 17th, and with so
much success, that Oudinot had resolved upon a
retreat for the next day, when he was wounded and
compelled to give over his command to St. Cyr,
who, on the 18th, suddenly assumed the offensive,
and compelled Wittgenstein to retreat, who now
took up a position behind the Drissa; so that the
strategical relations were not altered by this battle,
and both sides remained till October in mutual

observation, without any occurrence of importance.

From Riga the Russians under General Lewis, on the 23d August, made a strong sally on the Prussian right wing near Dahlenkirchen, drove it back with considerable loss, and retired the following day; after which nothing further took place till October.

On the French right wing, Schwarzenberg had united himself with Reynier, and had advanced against Tormasow. The latter had his right wing near Chomsk, his left at Pruschany. Schwarzenberg directed his whole force against this left wing. Tormasow left 12,000 men upon the Chomsk road, and attempted to withstand Schwarzenberg with 18,000 men, behind a marshy tract at Gorodeczna, between Kobrin and Pruschany. On the 12th August he was attacked by Schwarzenberg, who had turned his left wing. He maintained himself during the day, but was compelled in the night to begin his retreat to Kobrin. He continued it slowly to Luzk, where, on the 29th, he took up a position behind the Styr, while Schwarzenberg remained in his front. In this posture both sides remained till the arrival of Tschitschagow, which coincided nearly with the occupation of Moscow.

On the rear of the French, Marshal Victor had crossed the Niemen on the 3d September at Kowno with the 9th corps, 34,000 strong, and directed his march towards Smolensko, to form a central reserve.

FOURTH PERIOD. *From the occupation of Moscow to the retreat — from September 15. to October 23., five weeks.*

The French main army reached Moscow only 90,000 strong, and Buonaparte found himself in no condition to push his undertaking further. He wished to halt, and attend to proposals for peace, which, after the loss of a great battle and the capital, were to be expected from Russia.

The advanced guard alone, under Murat, from 25,000 to 30,000 strong, cautiously followed the Russian army; the other corps took up their quarters in the suburbs of Moscow, and the nearest villages on all the roads; so that the French army, according to the exigencies of their very advanced position, radiated with a front in every direction. Junot remained still at Mojäisk, but only with 2000 men; and in Smolensko, Baraguay D'Hilliers collected a division formed of battalions on their march, while Victor took up quarters between the Dnieper and the Dwina.

Such was the posture of the French for the first week, during which Murat in person followed the Russian army towards Riazan; Poniatowski was pushed forward on the Tula road towards Podolsk, and Bessieres on the Kaluga road towards Desna. Murat had pressed forward beyond the Moskwa, had there lost sight of the Russian army for two days, and then had drawn near it towards Podolsk, whence he manœuvred upon its right flank, while Poniatowski and Bessieres employed it in front; so that on the 26th September it was compelled to leave its position of Krasnoi Pachra, and retire slowly to Tarutino, where, on the 2d October, it took up an entrenched position behind the Nara, and remained there till the battle of Tarutino. These last movements were attended by daily affairs of rear-guard, which were occasionally very obstinate.

By this removal of the Russians to a distance of ten miles from Moscow, Buonaparte found himself in condition to extend his quarters in all directions from one to two marches from that city; while Murat, with the advanced guard, remained in front of Kutusow. Their position, however, on his flank, compelled him to place a couple of divisions on the Smolensko road, some miles from Moscow.

The Emperor of Russia had received, together with the report of the loss of Moscow, that of the gloomy position of the French army, and resolved to accept no peace. He foresaw the necessity under which Buonaparte would find himself of retreating before the commencement of winter. Already, at the period of the battle of Borodino, an instruction had been drawn up, by which Wittgenstein, Steinheil, and Tschitschagow were directed to unite in the rear of the French army, in order entirely to cut off their communications, and close against them the passages of the Beresina and Ula.

The Russian army was considerably reinforced at this period. The main army, which had passed the Moskwa only 70,000 strong, had been, by militia and troops of the line, raised to 110,000.

On the right wing Steinheil approached with 12,000 men from Finland, and Wittgenstein's force now amounted to 40,000. Around Moscow militia had been formed in all the neighbouring governments, viz. Moscow, Twer, Jaroslaw, Riazan, Wladimir, Tula, and Kaluga; who indeed, for the most part, were armed only with pikes, but who yet formed bodies considerable enough to force the French to show a front against them, and to be constantly on their guard.

Kutusow now felt himself impelled by his position to operate with strong detachments on the flanks. Already had Winzingerode, with a strong one of cavalry, been thrown forward on the French left, north of Moscow. A similar force was now detached under Dorochow on their right, which commenced operations by attacking the post of Wereja, hastily fortified by the French, and making prisoners of the garrison. All these advantages of the Russians could not be compensated by a reinforcement of 12,000 men which reached the French by degrees.

As no proposals for peace came from Petersburg, and already a fortnight had been wasted in inactivity, Buonaparte determined to make the first advance, and on the 4th October sent Lauriston to Kutusow with a letter for the Emperor Alexander. Kutusow received the letter, but not the bearer. Buonaparte suffered ten days more to elapse, and then renewed the attempt, beginning at the time to think on his retreat. Kutusow received Lauriston this time, which produced some specious negotiations, by which Buonaparte was misled to postpone his retreat for some days longer.

Exactly on the day fixed by Buonaparte for departure, Kutusow attacked the advanced guard under Murat. This body had taken up a position a mile from Tarutino, close in front of the Russians, nine miles from Moscow, behind the Czernicznia at Winkowo, without any intervening support. Murat was only 20,000 strong; his position bad; and 197 guns were rather an embarrassment than a help to an advanced guard. Kutusow by degrees became aware of this error, and attacked him on the 18th of October. He drove him back with a loss of from 3000 to 4000 men, and 36 guns, and then resumed his own position of Tarutino.

During this repose of five weeks at Moscow, the following events occurred in the other theatres of the war.

In Riga, September 20th, General Steinheil had landed from Finland with two divisions, together 12,000 strong. Strengthened by a part of the garrison, he took the offensive against the Prussians on the 26th; but after an obstinate action with General York, which lasted three days, and during which the siege artillery of the French at Ruhenthal was in great danger, he found himself compelled to retire, after considerable loss, to Riga.

General Steinheil proceeded immediately to effect a junction with Wittgenstein; but finding that the latter was on the point of assuming the offensive near Druja, he marched by the left bank of the Dwina, in order to attack Polozk from the rear. He reached the neighbourhood on the day of the action there, without being personally engaged in it.

At Polozk both parties, since the affair of the 17th and 18th August to the middle of October, had remained in face of one another without any occurrence of import. Wittgenstein's force at this time was increased to 40,000, and had the prospect of a junction with 12,000 more under Steinheil, while the force opposed to him was reduced to 30,000. Wittgenstein, induced by this superiority, and by instructions from St. Petersburg, resumed the offensive.

On the 18th and 19th of October, thus at the moment when Buonaparte was commencing his retreat from Moscow, Wittgenstein delivered the second battle of Polozk; won it; stormed the town, and forced the enemy to further retreat, the 6th corps (Wrede) retiring by Glubockoe to cover Wilna, the 2d by Czaswicki to join Victor. Wittgenstein sent detachments against Wrede, and pursued Oudinot slowly with his main body.

In the south, Tschitschagow, who on the 31st July had left Bucharest with the army of Moldavia, 38,000 strong, had effected his junction on the 18th September with Tormasow in the neighbour-

hood of Luzk ; and both together formed a force of
65,000 men, against Schwarzenberg and Reynier,
who were reduced to 40,000. Tormasow had the
command, and assumed the offensive. Schwarzenberg marched by Wladimir, on the left bank of the
Bug, down the stream; retired over it by Opalin to
Brezesc-Litewski, where the two armies found
themselves in presence on the 9th October. General Tormasow was called to the grand army ;
Tschitschagow advanced, on which Schwarzenberg
recrossed the Bug, and retired with the main army
on the Warsaw road to Wengrow, with the division
Siegenthal, to Byalystock. Tschitschagow declined
to commit himself further in advance; and having
received instructions to direct himself with a part
of his army on the Beresina, to embarrass the retreat of the French, he conceived that he had ample
time for that purpose, and withdrew his troops into
quarters for refreshment, in which they remained
to the end of October. General Hertel with one
hand from Mozyr kept the Austrian force at Pinsk
employed, with the other Dombrowski before
Bobruisk.

PART II.

*From the commencement of the retreat to the pas-
sage of the Niemen — from October 18. to December 11., seven weeks.*

This section requires no further subdivision; for
the retreat proceeds without any remarkable inter-

ruption, and preserves from beginning to end the same character, which only accelerates itself in its progress towards the entire dissolution of the army.

Buonaparte had set his army in motion the 18th October from Moscow, which he left himself the 19th, Mortier alone remaining there with the young guard.

As Kutusow from Tarutino had three marches less than Buonaparte to make to Smolensko, the latter thought it better to begin his retreat with a kind of renewed offensive, and to throw back Kutusow on the Kaluga, in order then to strike upon one of the side roads; for example, by Medyn and Juchnow to Doroghobusch. By such a manœuvre he would nullify the advance which Kutusow possessed over him before commencing his actual retreat; for from Malo Jaroslawetz, by his intended route, the distance is not greater to Smolensko than from Kaluga.

Buonaparte, therefore, marched at first on the old road from Kaluga to Krasnoi Pachra; turned then suddenly on the new road to Fominskoe; and by his advance on this threatened Kutusow's left flank and his communication with Kaluga, by which he probably hoped to manœuvre him back to Kaluga, even without a battle. Poniatowski was sent still further to the right to clear the way, and to recover the position of Wereja, which was effected on the 22d October.

Kutusow, however, although surprised by this unexpected movement, had time left him to push forward to Malo Jaroslawetz, where, on the 24th October, the two advanced guards met. Eugene, who commanded the French, had just time to place the Luja river behind him before he was attacked by Doctorof. The conflict was hot in Malo Jaroslawetz: both armies came up by degrees, but space was deficient to employ them. Eugene maintained his position, but could not move onward.

Buonaparte discovered from this very sanguinary affair that he could not manœuvre Kutusow back, and that it would cost him many men to effect that object by fighting. Although by the 25th he had assembled his army at Malo Jaroslawetz, he ventured on no fresh attack, and directed his retreat on the road by which he had come, namely, that of Borowsk, in order thence to strike again the Moscow road at Mojaisk. Kutusow on his part was as little disposed to a general action: he remained the 25th an half league from Malo Jaroslawetz, and made in the night a retrograde march on the Kaluga road to Gonczarowo.

The first day of the retreat, or rather that of suspension of fighting, the 25th, was distinguished by a bold irruption of Platoff at daybreak on the centre of the French at Gorodnia, by which eleven pieces of artillery fell into his hands, and Buonaparte himself narrowly escaped. On the same day other detachments of Cossacks showed themselves near Borowsk: this gave early occasion for fear of the Cossacks, and great anxiety for the events of the approaching retreat.

Mortier had blown up the Kremlin, and marched out of Moscow the 23d. He, with Junot, formed the advanced guard on the 28th between Gschatsk and Mojaisk, as Buonaparte reached the latter with the main body; and Davoust was still at Borowsk as rear-guard.

On the 31st, Buonaparte was with the advanced guard in Wiazma, the guards and Murat in Federowsköe, Poniatowski and Eugene in Gschatsk, the rear-guard under Davoust in Gridnewo; and thus the army extended some fourteen miles on the road.

Kutusow had moved on the 27th from his position of Gonczarowo, and advanced on the road which passes by Medyn and Wereja : he had marched down this to Kremensköe, and taken thence the direction of Wiazma. Miloradowitsch, however, marched with 25,000 men on Gschatsk, where he found the last French corps, which he stuck to; while Platoff followed them with 6000 or 8000 cavalry, and swarmed about them on either side with single detachments.

Buonaparte had halted two days at Wiazma to collect his army. On the 2d November he found himself with the guards, Murat, and Junot, at Semlewo, four miles from Wiazma; Ney at Wiazma; Eugene, Poniatowski, and Davoust at Federowsköe; so that the extent was only six miles.

On November 3d, Miloradowitsch and Platoff made a general attack on the corps at Wiazma, 40,000 strong: Kutusow came within a mile of

Wiazma to Vikowo, but took no part in the action.
The French corps, which had taken a position to
wait for Davoust, began their retreat upon his
coming up. They suffered much, but were not
cut off.

The occurrences from Wiazma to Smolensko
were as follows:—Two affairs of rear-guard, Ney
against Miloradowitsch, at Semlewo and Doroghobusch: the march of Eugene by Duchowtschina,
where he hoped to find more subsistence; but on
the 11th, at the passage of the Wop, he was forced
to abandon 60 guns, not being able to bring them
up the steep bank, and reached Smolensko with
great difficulty: the loss of an entire brigade of
infantry, 2000 men, under General Augereau, belonging to the division Baraguay D'Hilliers, who
had occupied Liskowa on the Jelnja road, and were
surrounded on the 9th November, and captured
by Orlow-Denissow and three other partisans: the
loss of 1500 oxen, collected near Smolensko for the
supply of the army, and which fell into the hands
of the Cossacks: finally, the first hard frost which
proclaimed the arrival of winter.

At Smolensko the French were melted down to
45,000 men. Buonaparte arrived there November
the 9th. His advanced corps only on the 10th.
He determined here again to halt for some days to
gain time for the distribution of the supplies at his
disposal: the delay in the arrival of Eugene's corps
obliged him to extend this halt to the 14th.

Junot and Poniatowski were with their corps,

1500 strong, one march in advance on the road to
Krasnoi, which is also that of Minsk.

The guards and Murat were in Smolensko; Eugene on the march from Duchowtschina; Davoust
was at Tschuginewo, four miles from Smolensko, on
the Moscow road; Ney as a rear-guard a mile further back behind the Wop. Eugene arrived on
the 13th; Davoust entered Smolensko; and Ney
remained at Tschuginewo, where he had to sustain
a hot affair with General Schacowskoi. Junot and
Poniatowski reached Krasnoi. Miloradowitsch, finding the subsistence of the troops on the great road
too difficult, and wishing also to go round the defile
of the Wop and Smolensko, had left General Schacowskoi on the main road with only a few thousand
men, and had marched with the rest upon Lioskowa,
by which he again approached Kutusow, who from
Wiazma had taken the direction of Jelnja, which
he reached on the 8th. Both now pursued their
march in the direction of Krasnoi.

Near Krasnoi, Kutusow had fully gained the
advance of the French army, so that it only depended on him entirely to obstruct their retreat,
for which the Dnieper afforded the greatest facilities; but Kutusow still feared his adversary, and
would not commit himself in a decisive battle, but
resolved to do him all the mischief he could without himself incurring the risk of a defeat. This
policy produced a succession of six actions in this
neighbourhood, which were highly destructive to

the French, although the latter appeared to come out of them as conquerors.

Junot and Poniatowski had reached Krasnoi on the 13th; Buonaparte with the guards had left Smolensko the 14th; Eugene, who had arrived the 13th, could only leave it the 15th; Davoust was to leave it only on the 16th, in order to remain near Ney, who was to enter Smolensko the 15th, destroy every thing there, and follow on the 16th or 17th.

1st battle of Krasnoi, November 14th: The guard fell, on the 14th, near Korytuja, upon a detached corps of Kutusow under Tolstoi Ostermann, from which it had to endure a heavy cannonade. —2d battle, the 15th: The guard found Miloradowitsch in position at Merlino, nearer to Krasnoi, and had to force their entrance into Krasnoi by hard fighting.— 3d battle, 15th: In the night Buonaparte directed an attack on General Ozarowski, who formed the head of Kutusow's column at Kutkowo, a mile south of Krasnoi, and drove him back with much loss. On this day Kutusow reached Szilowa, and thus was close in Buonaparte's front. — 4th battle, the 16th: Eugene, leaving Smolensko the 15th, reached Korytnja, and was to reach Krasnoi the 16th. He found Miloradowitsch already posted on the road. He himself was only 5000 strong, and found himself compelled, after a vain attempt at forcing a passage, to reach Krasnoi by making a circuit round the Russians; which he effected, but with considerable loss.—5th battle, 17th: Buonaparte fearing that Ney and Davoust

might fare no better, perhaps worse, resolved, while
Junot and Poniatowski were endeavouring to reach
Orsza, and Eugene Lidji, with the guard and
Murat to clear the way for his rearmost corps by
an attack on Kutusow, hoping to induce the latter
to draw off to himself the corps of Miloradowitsch.
He advanced, therefore, the 17th November, between Krasnoi and Kutkowo, with 14,000 men,
against Kutusow.

Kutusow, who thought the French main army
already passed, had resolved, exactly on this day, to
move forward on the offensive with his main body,
and to cut off every thing still in the rear. To this
end a column under Tormasow was ordered to
occupy the road to the left of Krasnoi, while he
himself advanced on its right. To strengthen, or
rather to unite his force, he called in Miloradowitsch to his right wing. As the action begun,
Kutusow perceived that he had to do with Buonaparte, and the main body of the army, which still
remained. He lost all desire to commit himself in
an action likely to prove too serious for his views;
and, satisfied that the French army must for the
most part perish, he halted Tormasow. The result
was some hours' undecisive firing; that Davoust
found his road open; and that Buonaparte marched
off towards Lidji. Davoust's rear-guard, however,
pressed by Miloradowitsch, suffered severely. The
Russians took on this day 45 guns and 6000
prisoners; 112 guns were picked up by the Cossacks, who pursued from Smolensko.

6th battle, the 18th : Ney was still behind. He had only left Smolensko early on the 17th, although Davoust had let him know that Eugene was half destroyed, and that he could not wait a moment longer to receive him. On the 17th he reached Korytnja ; on the 18th he fared like Eugene on the 16th. He was, like Eugene, about 6000 strong, and fell upon Miloradowitsch strengthened and extended to the left. Like Eugene, he made two attempts to break through, which failed; and convinced that a third could only end in his destruction, he resolved to attempt his escape by making a still greater circuit. He marched by night to the Dnieper; crossed its frozen waters at the village of Syrokorenie, not without the greatest difficulty; and then by Gusinöe, Komino, and Rasazna to Orsza, where he finally rejoined the main army, only, indeed, with 600 men under arms. The greater part of his corps, and his whole artillery, remained in the enemy's possession.

This was the last action which the French army had to sustain in gaining the advance of the Russians. The number of its men bearing arms was diminished perhaps by some 20,000; for it left Smolensko 45,000 strong, and reached the Beresina about 12,000, showing a loss of 33,000. A great part, however, of this total loss is to be placed to the account of fatigue, and the consequences of the actions, rather than the actions themselves. Some 10,000 stragglers fell also into the hands of the Russians in consequence of these contests, who might otherwise have followed the army further. We must therefore consider the results of these six actions as very influential towards the destruction of the French army, even though no entire individual corps was to be cited as having laid down its arms. The total number of guns captured in the four days, from the 15th over the 18th, amounted to 230.

On the 19th the French army, exclusive of Ney, was collected in the neighbourhood of Orsza, and the march was directed on the Minsk road. Since the loss of Witebsk, Minsk was the principal magazine. A great road led to it, and it was also the direction to which Buonaparte drew the nearest to Schwarzenberg. On these grounds he gave this road the preference over the direct route to Wilna by Malodeczno. The road to Minsk passes near Borissow, over the Beresina, which is encased for the most part in morasses: this point was therefore the next object of the march.

Events had mean while taken the following turn on the flanks : — Before Riga little occurred of consequence. The Russians still possessed a post on the left bank of the Dwina, between the Miss and the Aa. Their continual harassing of Macdonald's outposts induced him finally to drive them back to the right bank. He pressed forward on the 15th November with his principal column from Eckau on Dahlenkirchen, and cut off the right wing of the Russians, which was compelled, after the loss of some battalions near the village of Linden, to pass over the Dwina on the ice to the right bank. After this all remained quiet. Macdonald received official, but only general reports, of the retreat of the grand army, but none sufficiently disquieting to make him think of his own; orders for which he only received from Wilna on the 10th December, which he could not proceed to carry into effect before the 19th.

St. Cyr had retired after the 2d battle of Polozk upon Victor, who came to his support from Smolensko, and the junction took effect on the 29th October on the Lukomlia. The French were in consequence 36,000 strong, and somewhat superior to the Russians, who had been weakened both by casualties in action and detachments. Victor, who, in consequence of St.Cyr's wound at Polozk, had the command of both corps, Oudinot also not being yet recovered, considered it a duty to attack Wittgenstein, who had followed Oudinot's corps to Czasnicki, and made the attempt on the 31st October. In the middle, however, of its execution, he changed his resolve, and gave Wittgenstein the opportunity to attack with superior force, and to repulse with loss, the troops who had passed the Lukomlia; upon which Victor retreated upon Senno, and thence some days later to Czereja, which he reached the 6th November.

This removal of Victor to a distance from Witebsk induced Wittgenstein to detach thither General La Harpe with a corps, which on November 7th stormed the place, and captured the greater part of the garrison. As in this manner the magazines of Witebsk were lost to the French, it became pretty certain that the main army must retire upon Minsk.

Oudinot, recovered from his wound, had rejoined his corps; but Victor as the older marshal retained the command. As he reached Czereja he received from Buonaparte, then near Doroghobusch, the express command to attack Wittgenstein, and drive him over the Dwina. He therefore again advanced, and attacked the right wing of Wittgenstein pushed forward over the Lukomlia, and after a long struggle remained in possession of the village of Smoliany. Here, however, as he was only 25,000 strong, and found himself opposed to 30,000, as he perhaps thought more advantageously posted, a general attack seemed to him too dangerous, and he retired again to Czereja. In this posture both parties remained till the arrival of the main army in the neighbourhood of the Beresina decided their further movements.

Wrede, who had retired by Glubocköe to Danilowiczi, and had called in Corbineau's light brigade from Wilna, again advanced by Glubocköe, which he reached on the 19th November; while Corbineau joined Oudinot, fording the Beresina at Studianka, which had the consequence of inducing Oudinot to construct the bridges afterwards thrown over at that place.

In the south, Tschitschagow, after a fortnight's

repose, had put himself, on October 27th, in movement towards Minsk, leaving General Sacken, with
27,000 men, opposed to Schwarzenberg. He reached
Slonim the 6th November, remained there till
the 8th, and then pursued his march on Minsk,
which was defended only by 4000 men, but for
protection of which the division of Dombrowski
was in march from Bobruisk. On the 15th November, Tschitschagow's advanced guard routed a
detachment sent against him from Minsk towards
Nowoi Schwerschin. On the 16th he entered
Minsk before Dombrowski could reach it, who now
retired to Borissow.

Schwarzenberg, informed of Tschitschagow's departure, turned the left flank of Sacken, crossed the
Bug in the neighbourhood of Drohyczin, and followed Tschitschagow by Byalystock, Wolkowisk,
and Slonim, which he reached the 14th November.
Reynier covered this movement of Schwarzenberg
against Sacken by following the former as far as
Swislocz, and then forming a strong rear-guard in
Sacken's front. Sacken first fully understood the
movement of his adversary when the latter was
already over the Narew. He was then in the
neighbourhood of Wysoki Litewski, and hastened
after by Bialowies and Rudnia. Reynier faced him
again towards Rudnia, but retired before his superior
force to Wolkowisk, where he united himself with
the division Durutte, belonging to the 11th corps
(Angereau), which came up from Warsaw. He
informed Schwarzenberg, then in Slonim, in haste

of the advance of Sacken, and pressed him earnestly to return. Sacken fell on Reynier's head-quarters, November 15th, at Wolkowisk, and drove back the garrison with much loss. On the 16th he attacked Reynier's left flank, intending by a general action to force him away from Schwarzenberg: before, however, this could take a decisive turn, Schwarzenberg, who had left Frimont with 6000 men in Slonim, returned with his whole remaining force on Sacken's rear, compelling him to retire in haste, and with much loss, on Swislocz, and to continue this retreat, followed by Schwarzenberg and Reynier, by Brezesc Litewski upon Lïuboml and Kowel. Reynier followed upon Brezesc Litewski; Schwarzenberg on Kobrin, which he reached the 25th November. Here he received Buonaparte's orders to march on Minsk, and put himself in motion for it the 27th, the day of Buonaparte's passage of the Beresina. Reynier followed him December 1st.

Tschitschagow, released by Sacken from Schwarzenberg, moved on the 20th on the road to Smolensko towards Borissow. His advanced guard, under General Lambert, met with the division of Dombrowski at the *tête du pont* of Borissow. He attacked it, and drove it over the bridge with such loss that only 1500 men escaped, and retreated upon Oudinot, who on the 21st marched from Czereja upon Bobre, while Victor remained in Czereja.

Tschitschagow, on the 22d, pushed forward his advanced guard, under General Pahlen, towards Bobre as far as Losniska, crossed the Beresina himself with the army, and took up a position near Borissow.

At the moment, then, when the French main army, some 12,000 strong, quitted Orsza, the two Russian corps, which intended to close to it the passages of the Beresina and Ula, from which it was still eighteen miles distant, were at Czasniki and Borissow, some twelve miles apart; and the two opposed French corps upon the direct line from Orsza to these points, viz. at Czereja and Bobre.

Buonaparte, after losing Minsk and Borissow, had to think himself lucky if he could any where hit upon a passage of the Beresina, in order to take thence the direct route to Wilna. He was persuaded to abandon a hasty determination to cut his way to Lepel by an attack on Wittgenstein. He ordered Oudinot, therefore, to drive back over the Beresina such of the enemy as had crossed it from Minsk, and to take measures for the passage. He marched himself without delay on the Minsk road, and reached Bobre on the 23d November.

On this day Oudinot, who had moved forward from Bobre by Losnitza towards Borissow, had fallen on Tschitschagow's advanced guard under Pahlen, had driven it in with heavy loss upon the bridges, where Tschitschagow himself, in a state of inconceivable security, and unprepared for action, had barely time to regain the right bank and draw off Pahlen. Oudinot established himself in Borissow. On the 24th he reconnoitred the river, and made choice of the point of Studianka, two miles above

Borissow, for the bridge, while he made demonstrations at and below Borissow. The French had retained no bridge apparatus; so that the preparations for the two bridges lasted through the whole of the 24th and 25th, and the actual construction was only commenced at eight o'clock A.M. on the 26th, and finished at one. The neighbouring woods to some extent concealed the operation.

Tschitschagow thought it probable that Buonaparte would take his direction more to the south, as there he would draw nearer to Schwarzenberg. Starting from this too strongly conceived opinion, and confirmed in it by false reports which came from Kutusow himself, he considered Victor's preparations as demonstrations, and believed Buonaparte already on his march south. He therefore, on the 26th, just as the French main body reached Borissow, made a movement to the right towards Szbaszewicki, three miles from Borissow, on the Bobruisk road, while he drew away his left wing under General Tschaplitz from Wesselowo (Zembin) to Borissow, so that only a few Cossacks remained below that town.

Buonaparte was on the 24th at Losnitza, his rear-guard under Davoust at Bobre, Victor at Ratuliczi, Wittgenstein at Kolopodniczi. Kutusow, who had halted for some days after the actions at Krasnoi, passed, at the same time, the Dnieper at Kopius.

On the 25th Buonaparte reached Borissow, his rear-guard Krupki; Victor remained at Ratuliczi. Wittgenstein advanced towards Baran in order to approach Tschitschagow, and at the same time to obstruct the access to the Ula.

On the 26th, the remains of the French army were collected between Losnitza, Borissow, and Studianka, with a train of followers of twice its own numbers, without other artillery than that of Oudinot, Victor, and the guard, but with a mass of other carriages. The number of fighting men was about 30,000.

At one o'clock Oudinot crossed, and drove back General Tchaplitz, just then on his return, towards Stakow. Ney followed immediately; the rest remained in position on the left bank. Victor marched on in the evening of the 26th to Borissow, and Wittgenstein followed, but over cautiously, and only as far as Kostritza.

The passage was delayed by several failures of the bridges. In the afternoon of the 27th Buona-parte crossed with the guards, Eugene and Davoust in the night. On the 27th took place the first double conflict on either side the river. On the right bank, Oudinot and Ney had driven back the advanced guard of Tschitschagow under Tschaplitz to Stakow, one mile towards Borissow. Tschit-schagow himself returned from Szabaszcewitczi to Borissow. From fear of Buonaparte he did not venture to hasten to the aid of Tcshaplitz in force, but remained at Borissow, and sent only a rein-forcement.

On the left bank, Wittgenstein, who from excess of caution had taken the direction of Borissow, although he knew that the passage was at Studianka, fell on the division of Partonneau, left by Victor as a rear-guard at Borissow when he marched with the others to Studianka. Wittgenstein attacked this body, and forced it to lay down its arms to the number of 4000.

On the 28th, therefore, Victor alone remained on the left bank, and he with only one division. In order, however, to enable him to make a stand if possible for a day, and afford time for the passage of the mass of followers, the division Daendels of his corps was sent back. Now occurred the second double battle: on the left bank between Wittgenstein and Victor; on the right between the corps which had crossed and Tschitschagow, who now himself advanced, but could not press forward beyond Stakow. Both actions ended with the retreat of the French, but without the loss of any corps, and without putting it in Wittgenstein's power to prevent the destruction of the bridges. The French loss was, however, again very considerable; for Wittgenstein alone captured some 8000 or 1000 stragglers, exclusive of Partonneau's division. A quantity of guns and an enormous mass of baggage were also taken.*

---

* We must not be surprised to find baggage still with the French army. But a small portion of it came from Moscow; it was principally carriages of the country, which had been parked at Smolensko and other towns, and which were dragged on to the last, partly for transport of articles of subsistence, partly of plunder: they belonged generally to officers of rank.

As the dyke from Wesselowo to Zembin, which Wittgenstein as well as Tschitschagow had to pass, is a mile in length, and has several bridges which had been destroyed by the French, no immediate pursuit could take place except by means of cavalry detachments, which sought a passage through the marshes, and by fords of the Beresina. Both Tschitschagow and Wittgenstein sent out such to follow and accompany the enemy. Others had arrived from the main army, and joined in the pursuit. Wittgenstein occupied himself with repairing the bridge at Wesselowo, Tchitschagow with restoring those of the dyke.

The French army thus pursued its march upon Wilna, without being again overtaken by a Russian corps. General Tschaplitz alone, with the advanced guard and the above-mentioned partisan corps, remained near it, occasionally disturbing it from its bivouacks, and collecting the deserted guns and stragglers.

On the 29th, the French army was assembled between Zembin and Plesznicki. As Minsk was lost, it took the direct road for Wilna, by Malodeczno, Smorgoni, and Osmiana; while Wrede moved from Glubockoe on Dokcziczi and Wileika, and there fell into the road.

At Smorgoni, December 5th, Buonaparte gave over the command to Murat, and quitted the army for Paris, by way of Warsaw and Dresden. At Osmiana he met with the division of Loison, which, belonging to the 11th corps, had arrived from

Konigsberg to the relief of the army. It had suffered itself to be surprised by a Russian cavalry detachment under Colonel Seslawin, which it repulsed with difficulty, and Buonaparte himself narrowly escaped capture.

The army reached Wilna the 8th and 9th December, but as good as dissolved. The few marches which the division of Loison had made, and its contact with the main army, were sufficient so to disorganise it that, together with the corps of Wrede, it had but 2500 men under arms.

The guard still mustered 1500 men, the other seven corps but 300; the whole, therefore, about 4300 under arms, to whom were still attached about twelve guns. This weak remnant pursued their march with all possible haste to Kowno, which they reached on the 11th to the 13th, reduced to 1500, and without a single gun.

Tschitschagow followed on the great road to Wilna, which he reached on the 11th December.

Platoff followed close on the French to Kowno, which he reached on the 13th, and compelled them to continue their retreat by Gumbinnen, on the Vistula.

Tschitschagow followed some days later, and reached the Niemen on the 18th at Prenn. Kutusow had sent Miloradowitsch in pursuit, who, however, reached Borissow only on the 29th November, and thence marched by a side road to Malodeczno, where he regained the great road, fol-

lowed Tschitschagow, and reached Wilna the 13th
December.

The main army of Kutusow had marched on
Minsk, and thence to Wilna, where it took up cantonments on the 12th December.

Wittgenstein had marched to the right by Wileika on Niemenzin, and thence after some days'
repose by Wilkomir and Keidany to Georgenburg
on the Niemen, intending to cut off Macdonald.

The latter had broken up his force on the 19th
December into two divisions, a day's march separated, and marched by Janischki, Schawlia, Kelm,
Njemoktschy, Koltiniani, and thence partly by Tauroggen, partly by Coadjuten, towards Tilsit, where
General Grandjean arrived on the 27th, after having
on the 26th driven an advanced body of Wittgenstein's from Piktupohnen. Macdonald arrived with
another division the 28th, and waited the 29th and
30th for General York. The latter formed with
some 10,000 Prussian troops the 2d division, and
found on the 25th December at Koltiniani the road
occupied by another detachment of cavalry sent
forward by Wittgenstein under General Diebitsch:
the latter had pressed forward already some marches
further towards Memel, when he found that Macdonald was still behind, and expected at Koltiniani;
he therefore marched back, and hit by chance the
interval between the two columns. This gave occasion to the famous convention with York, which,
however, was only concluded after five days' nego-

tiation and short marches, near Tauroggen, on the 30th December.

Wittgenstein had pressed forward on this day already two marches from Georgenburg towards the line of Macdonald's retreat, and was at Gerskullen, tolerably near the road from Tilsit to Insterburg, and only one march from that which leads through the forest and by Labiau to Konigsberg, while Macdonald still remained in Tilsit. It was therefore easy for Wittgenstein to set himself in his way on the 31st. Wittgenstein, however, made on this day only a very trifling march; and Macdonald, who had broken up on the 31st from Tilsit towards Labiau, found only a couple of Cossack regiments on his way, and escaped, though with difficulty, and followed by Diebitsch and some other detachments.

He reached Konigsberg the 3d January, where he found the division Heudelet (belonging to the 11th corps), and with it pursued his retreat towards the Vistula, whither the other remnants of the grand army had preceded him. Wittgenstein followed Macdonald close, and indeed on his own responsibility, and by this drew the Russian army to a certain extent into Germany.

Schwarzenberg found himself till the 14th December in Slonim, in uncertainty as to the real state of affairs, as the victories gained by Buonaparte, according to his own reports, on the Beresina, led him to expect the near approach of Tschitschagow in full retreat. As soon as he had satisfied himself of the true situation of affairs, he commenced his retreat the 14th on Byalystock, and afterwards, threatened on his left flank from Grodno, gained Ostrolenka towards the end of December; while Reynier, followed by Sacken, went to Wengrow. Thus ended the campaign of 1812.

When the French army in the course of January had collected itself behind the Vistula, it found itself 23,000 strong. The Austrian and Prussian troops which returned mustered some 35,000 men; the whole, therefore, 58,000.

The allied army, inclusive of those who joined after the advance, had formed an effective of 610,000 men * ; 552,000 men had therefore remained in Russia dead or prisoners.

The army had brought with it 182,000 horses; of these 15,000 may have returned with the Prussians, Austrians, Macdonald, and Reynier. The artillery counted 1372 pieces ; the same corps brought back perhaps 150, so that more than 1200 were lost.

---

* According to Chambray, from whom the French numbers are taken. We gave at the beginning the French force at 440,000 men : in the course of the campaign there joined under Marshal Victor 33,000, with the divisions Durutte and Loïson 27,000, and others 80,000 ; together, about 140,000. The remainder were attached to the baggage.

Review of the Losses of the French Army of the Centre on the Advance and Retreat.

1. On the advance on the 24th June, the corps destined for Moscow were of the following strength:

1st	72,000 men.
3d	39,000
4th	45,000
5th	36,000
8th	18,000
The guards	47,000
Reserve cavalry	40,000
General staff	4,000
Total	301,000

2. At Smolensko, August 15th, the following corps were detached:

The division Dombrowski	6,000 men.
4th cavalry corps	5,000
Cuirassier division, Donmerc	2,500
Total	13,500

The army, therefore, should have been	287,000
Its effective force was	182,000

In 52 days, therefore, its loss was 105,500 men, which is about $\frac{1}{3}$d of the whole; dividing this by the number of days, we get the average daily loss $\frac{1}{150}$th of the original strength.

3. At Borodino, before the battle, were detached:

The division Dombrowski	6,000 men.
Laborde	6,000
Pino	10,000
Cavalry	5,000
Total	27,000

Deducting these detachments from the original
strength, 301,000, the force should have
remained - - - - - -   274,000
Real strength - - - - - -   130,000

Loss, therefore - - - - - -   144,000
which is about one half of the whole.

Thus this more recent loss of 38,000 in 23 days makes an average daily loss of $\frac{1}{120}$th of the whole.

The four actions of Smolensko are the cause of this increasing ratio of loss.

4. At the entrance into Moscow of September 15. :

Detachments.
Division Dombrowski -   -   -   6,000 men.
Junot - - - - - -   2,000
Cavalry - - - - - -   5,000

                          13,000

Original strength -   -   -   - 301,000

The army should have been -   - 288,000
It was - - - - -   - 90,000

Loss - - - - -   - 198,000
which is about $\frac{2}{3}$ds of the whole.

Consequently, the recent loss in 8 days of 54,000 makes an average daily loss of $\frac{1}{19}$th.

The battle of Borodino is the cause of this notable increase in the ratio of loss.

The result is, that, deducting the trifling amount of force detached, the French army of the centre reached Moscow with rather less than one third of its original numbers.

We have no reason to be surprised at the small amount of force detached. As far as the Dnieper and Dwina, Oudinot, St. Cyr, Victor (who arrived in September), and Schwarzenberg, with Reynier, were appointed to secure the rear. From Smolensko to Moscow regiments were, for the most part, taken on the march for garrisons for the few places important enough to require such on this line. In Smolensko, for example, Baraguay D'Hilliers formed a whole division of such troops. Among these certainly were a good many convalescents and stragglers, who are not to be reckoned as loss, but rather as detached; but their number was trifling in proportion to the whole, and, at all events, they were missing from the force at Moscow.

The causes of this enormous defalcation in twelve weeks of advance were the following: —

a. The uninterrupted movement in advance (120 miles in 81 days), which prevented all following of sick, wounded, or tired.

b. Continual bivouacking.

c. Very bad weather in the first five days.

d. Want of precaution in supply, which, so early as upon reaching Witebsk, caused the issue of flour in place of bread.

e. A very hot and dry summer in a country scantily watered.

f. The bloody and extravagant offensive tactic by which Buonaparte always endeavoured to overwhelm his adversary.

g. The great deficiency in hospital preparations, making impossible the recovery and restoration to their corps of sick and wounded, which, indeed, first showed itself during the great halt in Moscow.

THE RETREAT.

1. On the departure from Moscow, October 18th, the army was 103,000 strong. As the detachments had remained unaltered, the army had recruited itself in five weeks of its stay in and about Moscow to the amount of 13,000 men, which increase arose from convalescents and stragglers who came in during the period of inactivity; some fresh regiments also joined. The increase would have been greater, but for the losses incurred by sickness, and in procuring and bringing in supplies, as also the battle of Tarutino.

2. Wiazma, Nov. 3rd, before the battle:

The French army had left Moscow	- 103,000 strong.
It reached Wiazma - - -	- 60,000
Loss in 14 days - - - - -	- 43,000

$\frac{2}{3}$ths of the whole. Daily average $\frac{1}{35}$th.

The battle of Malo Jaroslawetz falls within this period.

3. Smolensko, November 10th:

The army was still 42,000 strong; had thus lost in eight days 18,000 men. Daily average $\frac{1}{26}$th.

The battle of Wiazma falls within this period.

4. On the Beresina, before the passage, November 26:

At Smolensko the army had found a reinforcement of 5000 men, and had reached thereby the amount of 47,000. Of these 10,000 came to the Beresina. Their loss, therefore, in sixteen days, was 36,000. Daily average $\frac{1}{20}$th.

The battle of Krasnoi falls within this period. The corps which came on from other parts to the Beresina, namely, the 2d and 9th, the division of Dombrowski, and the detached cavalry, had originally amounted to 80,000 men, and were now 19,000. They had thus in five months lost $\frac{3}{4}$ths of their strength. The army of Moscow, however, had, according to the above, lost $\frac{29}{30}$ths.

With the addition of these 19,000 Buonaparte was again 30,000 strong on the Beresina.

5. Three days after the passage of the river, and six after the 26th November, the 30,000 were again melted down to 9,000; making a loss of 21,000, and a daily average of $\frac{1}{8}$th.

The four battles on the Beresina fall within these six days.

6. Wilna, December 10th:

The above 9000 men were joined at Osmiana by the division Durutte, 13,000 strong; notwithstanding the army marched out of Wilna, December 11th, only 4000 strong. The loss in ten days, therefore, 18,000; daily average $\frac{1}{12}$th.

No battles in this period.

7. At the passage of the Niemen, December 13th, the remnant of the army was 1600 strong. The loss, therefore, in three days 2400; daily average $\frac{1}{5}$th.

The numbers here specified are those of men under arms. Stragglers and disarmed are not reckoned. The number of these increased so much down to the middle of the retreat, that near Krasnoi it was almost equal to that of the men under arms; from this period it decreased, and at the passage of the Niemen was very trifling. Generally speaking, very few of these stragglers recrossed the Russian frontier, which may be inferred from the circumstance that at the end of January, when the central army (exclusive of 10,000 men brought back by Reynier and Macdonald) was collected behind the Vistula, it amounted to no more than 13,000 men, including 2200 officers.

From this general view two results may be deduced, which have not yet been sufficiently noticed.

1. First, that the French army reached Moscow already too much weakened for the attainment of the end of its enterprise. For the facts that one third of its force had been wasted before reaching Smolensko, and another before Moscow, could not fail to make an impression on the Russian officers in command, the Emperor, and the ministry, which put an end to all notion of peace and concession.

2. That the actions at Wiazma, Krasnoi, and the Beresina, although no large bodies could be cited as cut off, occasioned enormous losses to the French; and that, whatever critics may say of particular moments of the transaction, the entire destruction of the French army is to be ascribed to the unheard-of energy of the pursuit, the results of which imagination could hardly exaggerate.

CHAPTER III.

FURTHER PROGRESS OF THE CAMPAIGN.

GENERAL BARCLAY left some 25,000 men under General Wittgenstein on the middle Dwina to cover the road to Petersburg, and, with the previous sanction of the Emperor, broke up from Drissa the 14th July, after an halt there of only six days, for Witebsk. There was unquestionably no time to be lost, as in point of fact the French might have been there long before him. It was only their protracted delay at Wilna which afforded him the possibility of making this flank movement to gain the Moscow road.

Barclay hoped in any case to be able to unite himself with Bagration. He had been promised a better position than that of Drissa ; he had at all events gained the Moscow road, and found reason to thank God for his extrication from the mouse-trap of Drissa. It was doubtless a misfortune to have weakened himself by the detachment of Wittgenstein; and the more so in respect of the great numerical inferiority of his force compared with that of the enemy, of which every day made him the more conscious. It was, however, reasonably to be expected that the French would leave behind a force in proportion to that of Wittgenstein; and under no circumstances could the responsibility be incurred of leaving entirely open the road to a capital the seat of the government of the country; for the French, with their enormous superiority of numbers, were able to detach a considerable force against Petersburg, which, in spite of its wide separation from the Moscow line of operation, would ultimately have reached its destination. A respectable force, however, left on this road, made such a project nearly impracticable; for it would have been swelled by reserves, militia, and such like, and the French must have started with a far greater force in order to reach Petersburg in sufficient strength. Barclay's view therefore, in making this sacrifice, was perfectly sound.

The army, nevertheless, found itself at Witebsk in a very perilous position; for it was already easy to foresee that Bagration would not arrive there; and the idea of a strong position there, even if such a position had existed, was inadequate to the circumstances. The march also upon Witebsk was neither more nor less than a flank movement of twenty-four miles, which must in itself be considered as an operation of great difficulty, as the French had already set themselves in motion, and had placed their centre at Glubocköe. The march was tolerably well secured by the Dwina; but at Witebsk it was necessary to pass over to the left bank, which might easily have been rendered impossible. The Russian army in this had great good fortune; and it is perhaps to be reckoned among the greatest errors of Buonaparte's career, that he did not draw greater advantage from the false movement of the Russians on Drissa.

The march to Witebsk was accomplished in ten days,—no great speed; but the Russians had learnt from their detachments of light cavalry that the French had not yet taken the direction of Witebsk.

Barclay, on arriving, marched through the town, and placed himself on the left bank of the Dwina, upon a rivulet which discharges itself into the Dwina near the town, so as to have its stream on his front, and the town on his right flank. The direction of this position was such, that the line of retreat, that is, the Moscow road by Poretsch, lay in the continuation of his left flank; but in his rear was the Dwina, at about a mile distance, which flows in a tolerably deep-cut valley at this place. A more detestable field of battle could hardly be imagined. General Barclay, on the day following his arrival, had pushed forward General Tolstoi Ostermann as an advanced guard to Ostrowno. This officer was attacked on the 25th by Murat, and suffered a considerable defeat; so that on the 26th Barclay was obliged to send forward a division under General Kannownitzin to his support. The whole drew back to within two miles of Witebsk. On this day the last corps, that of Doctorof, with the main rear-guard under General Pahlen, came up; and Pahlen was pushed forward as early as possible on the 27th to extricate the repulsed advanced guard.

We cannot clearly perceive why General Barclay

directed his march on Witebsk so leisurely. It was said at the time that the object was to afford time for the baggage to gain an advance.; this reason, and the indistinct notion of measuring his movements by those of his adversary, and of not evacuating more territory than was necessary, may have formed the grounds of this delay. This ill-timed composure, however, occasioned him a narrow escape from disaster.

It was, in fact, intended to wait at Witebsk for Bagration, whom they believed to be in the direction of Orsza; and if this were so, even to accept a battle. This idea was the *ne plus ultra* of indistinct conception; and we should term it madness, if the calm Barclay were capable of such. The Russian army, exclusive of Cossacks, amounted to 75,000 men; 200,000 might advance against it, and at the very lowest calculation 150,000. Should the position be turned by its left, which might be reckoned on with mathematical certainty, no further retreat was open; and the army would not only be forced away from Moscow, but might be entirely destroyed.

Barclay had already passed five days in this position, and every one conceived that it was his fixed determination to accept a battle in it; a course which, according to some, he had been anxious to adopt at Wilna, and had found objectionable only with reference to Drissa. The Author was in despair at this idea. The corps of General Pahlen, to which he was attached, had formed the rear-

guard from Polozk; but had scarcely come within
sight of the enemy, having for the most part
remained on the left bank of the Dwina. On the
26th, after a severe march, it reached Witebsk in the
night, and was obliged to move onward at daybreak
on the Senno road; being there reinforced up to
fourteen battalions, thirty-two squadrons, and forty
guns.

General Pahlen, with these forces, took up a
position some two miles from Witebsk, with his
right flank on the Dwina, and his front covered by
an insignificant rivulet. He placed his main force
of cavalry, not very judiciously, on the right wing;
because in that quarter, between the river and the
wooded edge of the valley, there was a small plain;
and a plain, according to received rules, is the
ground for cavalry. The space, however, was so
limited, that it was necessary to adopt a chess-
square formation in three or four ranks; and the
cavalry, in consequence, suffered much from the
artillery fire.

The high ground was occupied by infantry and
artillery. As, however, the fourteen battalions
were very weak, and mustered not more than from
3000 to 4000 men, and it was desirable to cover a
considerable space, in order in some measure to
protect the road, which was the more necessary
because the position had the deep-cut valley of the
Lutchesa in its rear, the result was a very thin
formation; in two lines, indeed, but with great
intervals between the battalions. Now the left

flank had no point of support; a natural defect, inasmuch as in so short a line it is rare to find such point for each wing. This, under the total want of reserves and depth of formation, made any manœuvre to turn the left flank one of serious danger to us. Things were made worse by the quantity of forest and brushwood in and in front of the position, which impeded the view. Under such circumstances the resistance could not be extraordinary; and if it lasted from five A. M. till three P. M., its duration can only be ascribed to the very languid advance of the enemy.

This last feature would be difficult to account for, since Buonaparte was with the advanced guard, and directing the attack in person, did we not know now that he believed the Russian army to be still in its position at Witebsk, and had prepared himself for a general battle.

Count Pahlen withdrew behind the Lutchesa, into the position which the army had occupied, and which General Barclay had evacuated the same day.

The latter had, in fact, when he found the French army approaching him in earnest, begun to feel apprehensive as to the position in which he had intended to deliver battle, and had changed his resolution at the last moment. We shall recognise him again frequently in this feature of his character. In this case it was an instance of real good fortune, and it may be said that the Russian army was here a second time saved from destruction.

The Author felt himself delighted, and in a frame of mind to thank God on his knees for thus having diverted our steps from the mouth of an abyss.

The action fought by General Pahlen left a very unsatisfactory impression on the Author's mind. The disposal of his force was not in accordance with the principles and views which the Author had formed for himself as to the handling of troops in action. Although the ground adjoining the crest of the height which rose from the valley was not, strictly speaking, open, yet it was not thick forest; and there was every where space for the movement of small detachments of cavalry, from a couple of squadrons to a regiment. The cavalry should therefore have been placed behind the infantry, which would have given greater depth to the formation; and from the whole mass a couple of regiments should have been used for observation on the left flank, and another couple for support of the infantry. In this manner the troops of different arms would have given each other mutual support, and the force would have been as strong again as it was on the high ground. On this high ground every thing depended; since the small level between it and the river, only some 600 paces in extent, might be commanded by the mere fire of artillery, and the enemy could not, generally speaking, penetrate between our position and the river.

As the Author had not been for above a week

attached to Count Pahlen, it was natural that he should have acquired but small influence with him; and Count Pahlen took up his first position without speaking with any one on the subject of it. The position once taken, nothing good could come of it; it is also next to impossible for a stranger, ignorant of the language, to exercise any active influence in the course of an actual conflict. Reports come in, discussions ensue, the orders are given, all in Russian; and the entire direction of an act of the transaction has taken its course, under the eyes of the said stranger, before he has heard a word of it. How can he, in such a moment, require a translation either from the commanding officer, or from any other well-informed person? Before he can look round he has lost the thread of events; and thus, even if he be a man of consequence, is void of means to make that consequence available. It was thus that the first battle, in which, by his station, the Author might have had some influence on the disposal of the force employed, was fought in a fashion directly opposed to his principles; and he felt himself so utterly useless, that he would rather have served as a subaltern in the line. It was therefore very agreeable to him when the reinforcement which Count Pahlen's force received on the 27th, after the action, brought with it an officer of higher rank on the general staff; so that the Author was at least no longer responsible for the consequences of dispositions over which he could have no influence.

Barclay marched on the 27th, in three columns, upon Smolensko; whither Bagration, after his ineffectual attempt to break through by Mohilew, had taken his direction. The march towards Smolensko was conducted with the main body on the Poretsch road, thus making a considerable circuit; Doctorof alone taking the direct route by Rudnia. It is inconceivable how Buonaparte omitted to throw forward his right wing, so as to cut off the Russians from this road. It is true that he would not thereby have closed to them the road to Moscow, for it is easy for a retiring party to gain the advance necessary for a small circuit; and if he can avoid finding himself thereby in a wrong direction, he cannot easily be cut off in an extensively open country. The Russians, however, had an important accessary interest in reaching Smolensko, in order to effect a junction with Bagration sooner than it could elsewhere have been managed. Smolensko might also hold out for some days. It contained considerable stores, and some troops; and it would therefore have been well worth while to have forced the Russians in a contrary direction. Buonaparte, however, pursued only as far as Rudnia, and made a second halt at Witebsk, during which he called in the last troops of his right wing, which had been destined to operate against Bagration, and, if possible, to cut him off. Thus the Russians gained time for the collection of their originally extended line at Smolensko, without losing any portion of it, and for making good the error of their false movement on Drissa. The movement to Smolensko was completed without difficulty; and the rear-guards of the three columns, although daily in sight of the enemy, had no actions of importance to sustain.

The result, then, of the campaign up to this period was, that the Russians had evacuated a territory of sixty miles in depth, with the sacrifice of all the magazines, and they were considerable, which it contained. In men and artillery, on the other hand, their loss was trifling; 10,000 men, perhaps, and twenty guns. They had now a great army in the centre of 120,000 men, and two smaller of some 30,000 each on the flanks; the fortresses also of Riga and Bobruisk had come into play: the latter in connection with the observation corps under General Hertel, stationed near Mozyr.

The French, on the other hand, had, in the first weeks of their advance, undergone an enormous loss in sick and stragglers, and were in a state of privation which gave early warning of their rapid consumption. This did not remain concealed from the Russians. General Schuwalow had been sent from Swanziany to the Imperial head-quarters on a political mission, and returned to Widzy full of astonishment at the state of the route of the French army, which he found strewn with the carcases of horses, and swarming with sick and stragglers. All prisoners were carefully questioned as to the matter of subsistence; and it was ascertained that already, in the neighbourhood of Witebsk, the horses were obtaining only green forage, and the men, instead of bread, only flour, which they were obliged to cook into soup. The guard alone was an exception. From this information the conviction was deduced of a considerable diminution of the enemy's force; and if this conjecture lagged far behind the truth, the error was neutralised by the circumstance that the enemy's numbers had been from the beginning estimated lower than the truth.

The French force, inclusive of its allied contingents, had been, on the commencement of hostilities, reckoned at 350,000. It amounted, as we now know, to above 470,000. It was known that some 150,000 had remained before Riga, against Wittgenstein, before Bobruisk, and against Tormasow. There remained then, on the Russian estimate, 200,000 for the main army: if 50,000 men were placed to the account of dead, sick, wounded, and stragglers, besides detachments for posts and garrisons, the Russian main army had to deal with no more than 150,000 men. This was still a preponderance, but not such as to put a victory out of the question.

The Russian calculation was not accurate; for Buonaparte's centre had, at this time, i. e. the beginning of August, still a force of 180,000 men.

This amount of error was excusable in a campaign in which the army was continually on the march, and had no time to receive many reports.

The command of the Emperor ceased with his departure from the army: Barclay was therefore independent general of the 1st army of the West. No formal command, however, of both armies, was assigned by the Emperor to Barclay, from an apprehension of mortifying Bagration. Barclay was, indeed, an older general in chief (general of infantry) than Bagration; and this circumstance was sufficient, in case of emergency, to give him authority over the latter: but for so weighty a charge as the command of an army the mere efficacy of a commission has never been considered sufficient, but in all services a special investiture by the sovereign has been held for necessary. As Bagration was not much younger than Barclay, and claimed something like an equality in military reputation, the Emperor foresaw clearly that an express subordination would be offensive to him. How the matter really stood as to the command, no one exactly knew, and I think that even now a writer would have difficulty in explicitly defining, without admitting that the Emperor had adopted a half measure. He probably recommended Bagration to come to an understanding in every thing with Barclay, pending any alteration in their relations. Whether at this time the nomination of Kutusow to the command of both armies was in contemplation, the Author is not aware; but in the army this appointment became matter of conversation only shortly before it took place, and was then spoken of as of a measure rendered necessary by the indecision of Barclay. The Emperor probably wished to see how Barclay would conduct himself, and to keep the subject open for another arrangement in due time.

On the arrival of Barclay at Smolensko, Bagration declared himself very ready to serve under his command, and the army was rejoiced at this harmony; it was, however, considered as unlikely to endure, for difference of views and dissensions soon arose.

Up to the period, however, of the junction, Barclay was, in fact, master of his arrangements. He had always an impression of a necessity of fighting; for the army saw with surprise the continual retreat. The effect was the more prejudicial, because the reports spoke of signal successes of the flank armies. Platoff's ambuscade at Mir, on the 10th July, had a brilliant appearance; Bagration's action at Mohilew, the 21st July, was taken for a victory on his breaking through the enemy; Tormasow's brilliant capture of the brigade of Klengel at Kobrin, the 26th July, had its full effect; and Wittgenstein's victory at Kliastitzi, the 26th July, was narrated without mention of the defeat sustained on the following day by his advanced guard, under General Kulniew. All this raised, at the first moment, the confidence and security of the troops; but this spirit gave place to complete mistrust, discontent, and languor, when they witnessed the continued progress of the retreat. No individual had originally anticipated or credited the possibility of retiring to Smolensko without a serious struggle. The junction with Bagration

became, however, an object too distinct and important not to be weighed as such, at least by most of
the officers of the Russian army.

As far as Smolensko, then, Barclay was sufficiently justified; but there every one felt the more
certain of a battle: that they were still too weak,
that by further retreat they would gain strength,
were ideas which occurred to no one. Barclay
himself had no distinct conception of them; and
if he felt himself rather held back than urged forward, it was more from the natural dread of the
decision of a moment, and the weight of its responsibility, than any internal clearness of conviction.

His general staff, Yermalof, namely, and Toll,
thought, in the general sense of the army, that
retreat had been carried far enough; that whatever
superiority in force still remained to the enemy
would be compensated by Russian valour and
Russian tactics. It was believed, especially, that a
sudden transition to the offensive would work
wonders. This is extant in all written accounts.
Bagration, who passed for a *sabreur*, and who,
after the fashion of such men, shook his head at
the hitherto negative results of the campaign, was
easily to be gained over to this idea. Colonel Toll
also used all his eloquence to persuade Barclay that
the moment was arrived for venturing on a decisive
blow. His arguments were these:—The French
main army was no longer so much superior to the
Russian. The first moment of the junction would
be the best for a sudden assumption of the offen-

sive. Smolensko was an important place; one much valued by the nation, and for which some risk was well to be incurred. The French army was scattered in extensive quarters, which afforded the fairest prospect of bringing them disunited to battle, and neutralising the superiority they still possessed. Great advantage belonged to the offensive; and the Russian soldier was more adapted for attack than defence.* It is known that all armies assert this of themselves.

Barclay suffered himself at last to be decided; and, on the 8th August, set his whole army in motion towards Rudnia, where he expected to find the principal force of the French central army.

On the first day's march, however, the report gained circulation that the French were on the road of Poretsch; and, under these circumstances, a stroke in the air in the direction of Rudnia was a serious matter, for no retreat would be open. Al-

---

* An opinion more at variance with the concurrent testimony of military historians and critics could hardly be cited, than this of Colonel Toll. If any nation be pre-eminent as an assailant, it is the French; if any distinguished for motionless obstinacy, it is the Russian. But we may be permitted to doubt whether their system of parade, accuracy in drill, and other details, have ever succeeded in giving their battalions that combination of steadiness and rapidity on which an arduous offensive operation must depend for success. Will it be considered as national vanity if we cite the English army as an happy combination of the two capabilities? Its obstinacy in defence was always beyond question; but the instances of its formidable qualities in attack are, if less numerous, not less conspicuous: Blenheim, Salamanca, Vittoria, Toulouse, and the sieges in Spain.

though this intelligence was not positive, and was rather the result of combinations and conjectures, and the incident it supposed was in itself improbable, as the Poretsch road was not at all in the direction hitherto adopted by the enemy, who had rather gained and threatened the opposite, namely, the right side of the Russian army, Barclay suffered nothing to prevent him from preferring certainty to chance, and from moving with the 1st army on the Poretsch road, while he left the 2nd stationary on that of Rudnia.

In the Russian army the abandonment of the offensive was the more regretted, because General Platoff, on the second day of the advance, before the order for a halt had been issued, had fallen upon the head of the advanced guard of Murat, under Sebastiani, at Inkowo, and taken the baggage of that general, and 500 prisoners, which seemed to promise the best results, as a good beginning to the whole. Bagration was also much discontented with the change of resolution, and from this period continual differences of opinion and contentions arose between him and Barclay.

Although this offensive of the Russians could hardly have led to a practical victory, i. e. to a battle, by the result of which the French could have been compelled at the least to forego their further advance, or even to make a considerable retrograde movement, it might yet produce a brilliant echauffourée, as the French are accustomed to term it. The French troops were, in fact, so disseminated over a great extent, that the retreat of such portions as the Russians should ·first fall upon became inevitable in the case of a rapid Russian advance. If the latter could only keep their three columns so near together as to admit of the execution of their commander-in-chief's orders on the day of their issue, it was possible to execute a comprehensive and successful attack on the corps immediately in their front, by which the enemy might incur considerable loss, independently of the smaller losses which might attach to the hasty movements, and the confusion more or less prevailing in the other neighbouring corps. The total result might then have amounted to some brilliant actions, a good number of prisoners, perhaps some guns; the enemy would have been thrown back some marches; and, which would have been the chief advantage, a good moral effect have been wrought for the Russians, and the reverse for the French. These advantages, however, once reaped, the Russians would unquestionably have been com-. pelled either to accept a battle with the entire French army, or to recommence their retreat. If a voluntary retreat into the middle of European Russia had been the main feature of a system, such further retreat would have been entered upon without hesitation, and the transaction would have come under the category of a great sally from a fortress. Of such a view, however, no indication was apparent in those who managed the war; and it is not to be doubted that, after the first advantages of the offensive, they would have held themselves obliged to make further head against the united force of the enemy, in order to avoid the appearance of having been defeated; and thus it is most probable that after a success the next result would have been a great defensive action, of which the consequence could hardly be doubtful, when the relative proportions of the forces engaged are considered. This probably presented itself vaguely to the contemplation of Barclay, and was little inviting; least so when he came to consider the possibility of being outflanked.

It was thus that the affair appeared to ourself at the time, and we have since seen no reason to change our view. A general who had the idea of a protracted retreat distinctly before him,—who was penetrated with the conviction that in war we must act much on probabilities, and have courage enough to leave something to fortune, would, on the 9th August, have gone boldly forward, and tried his fortune with the offensive for a couple of days; but a general like Barclay, who looked for the salvation of the cause only to a complete victory, who considered it his duty to seek for this only in a regular and previously arranged battle, who listened to the voice of external (objective) reasons the more that the internal (subjective) remained silent,—such a man, before he gives up his original scheme, must have found more than sufficient reasons for such abandonment in a concurrence of all the circumstances of the moment. The views of Colonel

Toll, and those officers of the staff who most eagerly advocated the continuance of the enterprise, were, that by a sudden offensive, and by the surprise of the enemy while disunited, the victory would be at once achieved, ˉand the enemy *culbute*. Such expressions are merely mischievous in the art of war, as possessing a species of terminological force, yet, in fact, being destitute of any distinct ideas. According to all historical experience, such surprises in strategy seldom produce a positive victory, but merely an acquisition of ground, and a favourable introduction to a battle. For to a regular victory it is essential that a respectable portion of the enemy's force should be reached, brought to blows, and hemmed in, and a mere repulse, which may pass justly for a victory when the whole is involved, cannot constitute such when it affects only a part of that whole. Now the separate corps of an enemy seldom make a stand; most of them attain, by forced marches to the rear, a rallying point; and one seldom finds, except under circumstances of extraordinary geographical advantage, opportunity to strike a really effective blow. The enemy doubtless, by such a surprise, is placed in a worse position than before, but not in that of a beaten whole; and if the assailant was not before strong enough to risk a general action, he will hardly have become so by such a partial success. That the choice of position, knowledge of the ground, and possible assistance of field works, give the defensive party in a battle many advantages, is a natural and evident rule, where the idea of the defensive is clearly established, and every thing accordingly in its proper posture; but in 1812 the offensive form was a pure arcanum, since the French, who were to be sought out and attacked, were the superior party. Whoever investigates the subject will say to himself that the offensive form is the weaker, and the defensive the stronger, in war; but that the results of the first, when successful, are positive, therefore the greater and more decisive; of the latter only negative, by which the equilibrium is restored, and one may be advocated as well as the other. From this digression, which has led us rather deeply into theory, we return to General Barclay.

Of the campaign, as it afterwards evolved itself in the shape which alone admitted of so complete a catastrophe as occurred, the offensive now contemplated was no essential component; and if it was to terminate in the loss of a battle, it was far better that it should be totally omitted, since, in any case, it was to be foreseen that in seven weeks a victory would be possible, or even probable, and seven weeks might be occupied between this and Moscow.

Those about Barclay meanwhile renewed their efforts to persuade Barclay to the offensive; and, in fact, after remaining four days on the Poretsch road, he made, on the 13th and 14th, two marches towards Rudnia; but it was too late. The French, roused from their quarters by the first attempt at attack, put themselves in motion for a fresh advance; and, passing the Dnieper at Rasasna on the 14th, moved upon Smolensko. This called Barclay first, and afterwards Bagration, to Smolensko; for already had the division of Niverowsky, which had been sent forward against the enemy to Krasnoi, sustained a disadvantage, and thrown itself into Smolensko.

This town, one of the most considerable in Russia, with a population of 20,000 souls, had an ancient wall, something such as that of Cologne, and a bad and ruinous earthen work on the bastion system. The position of Smolensko is so unfavourable for a fortress, that it was only with great expense it could be made into a place worth occupying and arming. It lies, in fact, upon the declivity of the high margin of the river on its left; so that from the right bank the place and the lines which descend to the river are strongly overlooked, although this right side is not higher than the left. This position is the reverse of a good one, and is a specimen of the worst shape of being commanded. It would therefore be a very false judgment to pronounce that the Russians might, with a little trouble, have made Smolensko into a fortress: into a place which might have held out eight, at the highest fourteen days,—granted; but it is clear that, for so trifling a resistance, a garrison of from 6000 to 8000 men, from sixty to eighty guns, and a quantity of other articles, would have been too great a sacrifice.

As Smolensko was, it could only be defended *a force de bras ;* but in this case would cost many men to the storming party.

For the Russians Smolensko had this value, that it contained their magazines for present use. So long, therefore, as they intended to remain in its neighbourhood, it was natural that they should be ready to fight for its possession. Bagration hastened, therefore, on the 16th, to occupy it with a a corps of fresh troops.

Barclay knew not properly, at this moment, whether his own head was on his shoulders. In virtue of the continued intention to act on the offensive, the preparatory measures towards a good position for a defensive battle had been delayed. The Russians were now thrown back on the defensive; had no clear idea where and how they should place themselves; and would probably have resumed their retreat at once, if Barclay had not turned pale at the thought of what the Russians would say, if he, in spite of the junction of the two armies, should abandon this half-canonized town without an action.

The neighbourhood of Smolensko is essentially unfit for a defensive position, for the direction of the river is in this neighbourhood that of the line of operations; and, in addition to this, the road to Moscow, near Smolensko, *i. e.* a league higher up, runs close to the river. If, therefore, it be intended to meet the enemy with a parallel front, and to have one's own line of retreat perpendicular to the rear, it would be necessary to take position on both sides of the river, and therefore to take the town either before, behind, or into the front line, which would be a very defective position; as the communication for an army, especially a weaker one, over two bridges, and through a tolerably extensive town, could not be an advantageous one. In any position confined to one side of the river, the line of retreat would be in jeopardy. On the left bank, moreover, it would be impossible; for the army would then have the Dnieper, which makes above the town an angle to the south of ninety degrees, behind it at half a mile distance, and the whole French army was already on the left bank. All this increased Barclay's difficulty. He determined therefore, in the first instance, to do that which was most urgent,— to let Bagration march off with all haste to Smolensko on the 16th, the corps of Rajefsky having been sent there the day before, and to follow in person with the 1st army. General Rajefsky united himself on the 15th, in Smolensko, with the division of Wiewerowsky; and the two formed a garrison of 16,000 men: enough to secure the place for the moment, and to resist a preliminary attack of Murat and Ney on the 16th. Barclay, however, felt further that it was urgent also to secure the line of retreat. He therefore detached Bagration, early on the 17th, to Valutina Gora, on the Moscow road, one mile from Smolensko, a place where the direction of the road diverges from that of the river; so that the disad-

vantage of the propinquity we have mentioned
ceases. Here was then the point where it would
have first been possible to take up a position above
Smolensko. It was, however, too far from the
town to enable its occupant to hold the latter, and
to include it as a tactical portion of the whole.

After taking these measures, Barclay determined
to occupy Smolensko with the 1st army, and to
wait for the further operations of the French. This
resolution was not ill-conceived; for, as the French
were so obliging as to place themselves with the
entire of their enormous force on the left bank of
the Dnieper, the two armies remained separated
by Smolensko and the valley of the river; and the
retreat of Barclay lay, it is true, on the left flank,
but covered by the position of Bagration. Barclay,
so stationed, was able to wait quietly till the French
should either take Smolensko, or be making preparations to cross the river. The French were
complaisant enough to begin with the former; and
thus arose, on the 17th, the second battle for the
possession of Smolensko, in which Barclay by
degrees supported Doctorof with three divisions
and a half of fresh troops, so that the Russians
brought into action about 30,000 men. Both
armies looked on, without being able to take part in
the action. Doctorof fought for the most part in
the suburbs, since the walls and works had not the
requisite banquettes and steps for mounting. This
occasioned him a great loss of men; but it was in
the nature of the action that the French loss should

be still greater. The Russians in the suburbs were finally overmastered by superior forces, and driven into the town. The defence was hereupon nearly exhausted; but evening closed in, and the French were not in possession of Smolensko on the 17th, for some attempts to batter the city wall failed at the moment. Barclay had now attained his object, which was, in fact, entirely local; namely, not to abandon Smolensko without a struggle.

The defence of Smolensko was, in truth, an extraordinary transaction. A general battle was out of the question; as the Russians, after the loss of the town, would obviously decline such, having detached one third of their force with Bagration to the rear. Should they not lose it, they would never be able to break out from this point against the French; as it is not to be conceived that the army of the latter could be exhausted against the walls of the place, and become the instruments of their own defeat. A partial conflict then alone could be the result, which could effect no alteration in the general proportions of the respective parties, and therefore could not alter the advance of the one and the retreat of the other. The advantage to Barclay was, that it was a contest which could not lead to his total defeat, as might easily happen in a serious struggle with a superior adversary. He had it in his power to break off at any moment, at the price of abandoning the town. The second advantage was, that the Russians in the suburbs were more protected than their adversaries, and had

a secure retreat behind the walls of the town.   The
mere military result was, that the French lost many
men, some 20,000, while the Russian loss was less;
and that in the condition which things had now
reached, this loss of the Russians could be more
easily replaced than that of the French.   Where
the object is to conduct with advantage a defensive
retreat into the far interior of a country, a continual
resistance is a very essential part of such system, in
order that the enemy may consume his strength
against it.   In this sense, then, the battle of Smolensko is a valid portion of the campaign, although
by its nature it could not be efficacious for a total
conversion of the previous relative situation of the
parties.   That it had for Barclay a special value
with reference to the Russians, and that this was
the actively impelling principle of the measure with
him, we have already said.

On the evening of the 17th arose the question,
whether Smolensko should be further defended.
The reports of General Doctorof were not calculated to produce an affirmative decision.   The
town itself was partly burnt down, and still in
flames; the ancient fortifications were not adapted
for defence; the two corps which had fought there
were, by the enormous loss in action, some 10,000
men, a third of their original strength, much
weakened: should the French attack by storm, and
succeed, another third might be sacrificed; and in
this case the loss would exceed that of the enemy,
as the circumstances would then embrace the

making of prisoners. The advantages and relations, therefore, which existed on the 17th, existed now no longer; and Barclay determined to weaken himself no further, but to abandon that part of the town which lies on the left bank, to withdraw to the suburb on the right bank, and to destroy the bridge. This was effected in the night of the 17th.

With this resolution General Barclay should have combined that of retreating on the 18th, and uniting together with Bagration on the Moscow road. This resolution, however, was not adopted till the 18th; and, on that day, it was thought too hazardous to commence the march, which was a regular flank movement, by open day, in the sight of the enemy, especially as the latter had already made some attempts to cross the river, which were, however, repulsed. Barclay preferred, therefore, to remain quiet the 18th, and to commence his retreat after dark in two columns, and by a circuitous route, by marching first a certain distance on the Poretsch road, that to Petersburgh, and then turning short to that of Moscow, which he purposed to hit at Lubino, two miles from Smolensko. A detachment of some thousand men was ordered to retire under General Tutschkow, on the direct Moscow road, till it should reach the extreme rear-guard of Bagration. Bagration himself had broken up on the 18th from his position at Valutina Gora, towards Doroghobusch. General Korf, with a strong rear-guard, was to remain at Smolensko, and cover the movement.

The determination to wait till dusk was unavoidable, as they had delayed commencing the retreat in the previous night; but the dispositions adopted were not to be praised.

As the great road to Moscow was as yet quite open, and General Tutschkow was able to move on it with a detachment of all arms, we cannot perceive why General Barclay did not shorten his own column by sending two corps on this road. These two would have been able to avail themselves of the frequent hollows which intersect this road at right angles, to make resistance sufficient to allow the other column to make good its circuitous route. It is our belief that Colonel Toll involved himself here a little in the subtleties of staff-officer science: we heard, at least, much laudation afterwards of the scientific detour of the army.

We have hitherto, with respect to the battles of Smolensko, spoken only of Russian motives; but we cannot avoid dwelling for a moment on those of the French. We confess that we here alight upon the most incomprehensible passage of the campaign. Buonaparte found himself on the 7th, when Barclay made his attempt at the offensive, with his 180,000 men, for the most part between the Dnieper and the Dwina: Davoust alone had crossed that river at Rasazna, with 30,000. It was easier then for Buonaparte, and more natural, to advance on the Witebsk road to Smolensko, than on that of Minsk. Smolensko, moreover, was plainly no object of operation to him, but the Russian army was; which, from the beginning of the campaign, he had in vain endeavoured to bring to action. That army was now in his front: why did he not collect his troops so as to advance straight upon it? It is further to be observed, that the road from Minsk to Moscow, by Smolensko, on which Buonaparte now moved, crosses over the Dnieper to its right bank at Smolensko; and that Buonaparte, therefore, had to recross that river. Had he met Barclay directly, the latter would scarcely have been able to retire to Smolensko, and certainly could not have paused there, since the French army on the right bank would have threatened the Moscow road much more effectually than from the left, where the town and the river, for a space, covered that road. Under these circumstances Smolensko would have fallen without a blow; Buonaparte would not have sacrificed 20,000 men, and the place itself would probably have been saved, as the Russians were not yet so expert in the burning system as they afterwards became. After Buonaparte had arrived before Smolensko, it is again not easy to conceive why he insisted on taking it by assault. If a respectable force had been sent across the Dnieper, and the French army had made a demonstration of following it, and placing itself on the Moscow road, Barclay would have hastened to anticipate it, and Smolensko would have fallen without a blow. If this was not a case in which, by a mere demonstration, all the advantages of an action might have been gained,

that is, in which the enemy might have been manœuvred out of his position, there is no such thing
as manœuvre in war. We know of no solution for
this conduct of the French commander, and can
only look for one in the local difficulty of the collection and subsistence of the army, and the superior convenience of the greater road, which may
have led, in the first instance, to a false movement;
and when Buonaparte arrived before Smolensko, he
wished, perhaps, to astonish by a *coup d'éclat*.
This, in our opinion, is the third and greatest error
committed by Buonaparte in this campaign.

We leave now the neighbourhood of Smolensko;
and on the battle of Valutina Gora we dwell merely
to remark that Barclay here distinguished himself
by that which was his best quality, and the one
which alone justified his selection for an important
command; namely, a perfect composure, firmness,
and personal bravery. So soon as he found that
General Tutschkow was pressed too strongly on
the great road, to allow him to make good the
time which the circuitous march of his own column
required, he betook himself in person to this rear-
guard, drew from the nearest column the first
troops he could command, and thus, on very advantageous ground, delivered again a partial action,
which cost the French at the least as much as the
Russians, who reckoned their loss at 10,000 men.
This battle had become unavoidable for Barclay,
but it was not an unavoidable evil; for bloody
struggles with the enemy were essentially in the

part he had to play.   It would only have been an
evil, if the special object of the action, the covering
of his flank march, had not been obtained, and a
part of his army had been cut off.

The Russians lost in these actions some 30,000
men; we may, however, reckon that between this
and Borodino, they were reinforced by 20,000; so
that the diminution only amounted to 10,000.
The French were 182,000 strong at Smolensko,
and 130,000 at Borodino.   Their diminution,
therefore, reached 52,000, of which 16,000 were detached, namely, the division of Pino, which marched
to Witebsk 10,000 strong, and that of Laborde,
who remained in Smolensko with 6000.   The loss
of the French, then, in these actions, and in sick
and stragglers, was 36,000.

Thus the two armies converged towards the
point of equalisation.

The actions of Smolensko, which, as we have
seen, took a shape and turn quite conformable to
the views of Russia as to the campaign, had so
moulded themselves out of incidental circumstances,
and without any distinct consciousness on the part
of the Russian chiefs.   The continuation of the
retreat on the great road arose out of the mere
pressure of circumstances.   Barclay was, in his own
mind, any thing but satisfied with the results of his
exertions at Smolensko, although obliged to appear
as if he considered them a half victory.   He was ill
at ease, and felt it as a load on his conscience, to be
approaching Moscow without having, by a general

and arranged battle, attempted to convert the advance of the French either into a halt or a retreat. His staff felt the urgency of such a battle still more strongly. The resolution was therefore adopted, to concert and deliver a regular defensive battle in the first good position which could be found on the Moscow road. The first which presented itself was at Uswiate, behind the Uja, a mile west of Doroghobusch, at which the army arrived on the 21st. Colonel Toll, who usually preceded the army one day to take up the ground for the next, had discovered here a field of battle, which appeared to him to promise the best results. The Author, who at this time was in Colonel Toll's company for several days, had occasion to learn his ideas on the subject with certainty. The position was, in fact, very advantageous, but we can hardly say very strong. With the right wing on the Dnieper, it had a small stream, the Uja, in front. This stream is insignificant, and does not flow in a deep valley, but nevertheless presents some difficulties of access; and the smooth slope of the banks was very favourable for the effect of the Russian artillery. In front the ground was open every where, and well overlooked; in rear it was more covered, and gave facilities for concealing our own formation. The 1st army alone was destined for its occupation; the 2d, under Bagration, was intended to act as a reserve, a league to the rear, towards Doroghobusch, and in *echelon* behind the left wing of the 1st. By this concealed position of Bagration, it was hoped to effect the covering of the left wing, which had no point of support, and to gain means for an unforeseen offensive. This seems to have been a favourite notion of Colonel Toll, for we find the same measure adopted at Borodino with the corps of General Tutschkow strengthened with militia, though on a smaller scale, for Tutschkow was far inferior in force to Bagration, and placed much nearer to the front. The Author had always considered such an arrangement as eligible in principle; for in his view a wing, which has no natural strength of ground to lean on, can only be covered by reserves of proportionate strength, which may assume the offensive, more or less, according to circumstances. The Author, therefore, entered the more readily into Colonel Toll's ideas, and thought, if we are to fight to-day or to-morrow, better here than elsewhere.

General Bagration, however, was greatly dissatisfied with the position; a little hill which rose in front of the right wing beyond the Uja was considered by him as a domineering eminence, and as a cardinal defect. Colonel Toll, who was very obstinate, and not very courteous, was unwilling to give up his idea at once, and ventured on a controversy, which threw Bagration into a violent passion, and produced from him a declaration not unusual in Russia, " Colonel, your behaviour deserves for you a musket across your shoulders." As this figure of speech in Russia is not a mere *façon de parler*, but as, according to the rules of her service, a kind of degradation can occur, by which the most dis-

tinguished general can, at least in form, be reduced
to the ranks, the threat was not altogether to be
despised. Barclay, who could not have supported
his quarter-master-general, unless he himself had
been prepared to fill in every respect the place of
commander-in-chief, and could have enforced silence
and obedience on the part of Bagration, was far
enough from doing so, for it was practically impossible for him to exercise such authority, and
his character and habits were too little those of
a master. Neither is it to be doubted, that his
courage for action sank in proportion as Buonaparte approached. The two generals agreed to
abandon the position so much extolled by Colonel
Toll, and on the 24th to take up one further to the
rear near Doroghobusch, which Bagration considered
one of far greater advantage.

This position was, in the opinion of the Author,
detestable. In front it presented no difficulty of
access and no clearness of view—the town of
Doroghobusch, extensive, angular, and hilly, behind
the right wing, and a part of the troops, namely, the
corps of Baggowut, in a still worse position on the
other side of the Dnieper. The Author was in
despair at this change, and Colonel Toll in sullen
fury. Fortunately the resolution did not last long,
—in the night of the 24th the army again retired.
Four marches took place in this manner, always
with the view of accepting a battle in the next
position, and always with the result that the position, when reached, was abandoned.

The next reinforcement which was to be expected, a reserve under General Miloradowitsch, which was intended to consist of 20,000 men, but only amounted to 15,000, and on which we had reckoned so long ago as at Uswiate, arrived on the 27th at Wiasma.

On the 29th Barclay believed that he had really found, one mile short of Giatsk, a position which, with the aid of contemplated improvements, would warrant the risking a battle. He strengthened it immediately with some works. On this day, however, Kutusow arrived as commander-in-chief ; Barclay assumed the command of the 1st army, and Kutusow forthwith continued the retreat.

This change of commanders had become a topic of conversation in the army but a few days before it took place, a proof that Kutusow's appointment had not been arranged immediately on the departure of the Emperor. Kutusow, in such case, would have arrived earlier. It was believed in the army, that the indecision of Barclay, which prevented him from coming to a regular action, and the mistrust which ultimately prevailed against him as a stranger in the army, had at last decided the Emperor to place at the head of the army the man among the true Russians who had the most reputation.

If we look to dates, it will appear as if the abandonment of the offensive at Smolensko was what decided the transaction. It took place on the 7th and 8th, and three weeks later Kutusow arrived. It is probable that in the interval many reports reached Petersburgh unfavourable to Barclay, and the principal agent in these was probably the Grand Duke Constantine*, who was still with the army at Smolensko, and was completely won over to the idea of the offensive. These reports must have reached Petersburgh by the middle of August; and it is thus explained, how General Kutusow with a little exertion could join the army a fortnight later.

In the army there was great joy on his arrival. Up to this time every thing, in the opinion of the Russians, had gone very ill; any change, therefore, was held to be for the better. The reputation of Kutusow, however, in the Russian army was not very great; at least there were two parties on the subject of his claims to distinction: all, however, were agreed, that a true Russian, a disciple of Suwarow, was better than a foreigner, and much wanted at the moment. Barclay was, in truth, no foreigner; he was the son of a Livonian clergyman, a native of that province; he had served from his youth in the Russian army, and there was therefore

---

* If the following anecdote, which we have heard on good authority, be true, the service, which the Author supposes Constantine to have rendered to Kutusow, was ill requited. The former is said, on a subsequent occasion, to have complained to Kutusow of neglect and want of confidence. Kutusow replied, that he was anxious to consult his wishes, and would in the first instance entrust him with a dispatch of the first importance to the Emperor. When the Grand Duke and the dispatch reached Petersburgh, the latter was found to be a sheet of blank paper, and its bearer returned no more to the army. — T

nothing foreign in him but his name, and perhaps, also, his speech; for he spoke Russian ill, and was more accustomed, by preference, to the German language.   This was sufficient to make him, under present circumstances, be considered a foreigner. That the Lieutenant-Colonel Wolzogen, who had been but for five years in Russia, remained about General Barclay without the post of adjutant, or any situation on the quarter-master-general's staff, caused him to be considered as an intimate councillor of Barclay, and placed the imputed foreign character of the latter in a stronger light.   Wolzogen himself, who had a serious exterior, and not one of that insinuation which is required in Russia, was persecuted with real hatred.   The Author heard an officer who returned from head-quarters pour out his bitterness, and say of Wolzogen, that he sat there in a corner like a fat and poisonous spider.

As according to Russian opinions every thing went as ill as possible, the evil was all ascribed to the traitorous counsels of this stranger; it was not doubted that Barclay followed, in every thing, his secret suggestions.   The ill-will and distrust with which Toll and Yermaloff treated him, from believing that he sometimes opposed their views, and had done much mischief by his bad advice, probably gave the chief impulse to this disposition towards Wolzogen.   The abandonment of the offensive at Smolensko was cited against him, because he had principally held the opinion, that the main force of the enemy was on the Poretsch road. They did him, meanwhile, much too great honour in ascribing to him as much influence as they did with Barclay. Barclay was a rather cold man, not very susceptible of suggestions; and with such characters, the surrender of themselves to others is not usual; neither was Wolzogen satisfied with General Barclay, or with the part he had to play, and was only content to support it because he thought he might do good in particular instances, or prevent mischief.   Least of all, did he deserve the misconstruction which his intentions underwent.   It was a trait of the Tartar character to consider as a traitor an officer, one of the Emperor's aide-de-camps, and in his confidence, without one reasonable ground, merely on account of his name.   This suspicion of foreigners was first aroused against Barclay and Wolzogen, and extended itself among the ruder portion of the army, by degrees over all other foreigners, of whom, it is notorious, there are many in the Russian service. Many Russians who did not attribute treachery to the foreigners, yet believed that the household gods of their country might be indignant at their employment, and that it was therefore unlucky. This was, however, only a suppressed feeling on the subject in general, and is mentioned here because it is characteristic of the people, and shows what was the current of opinion with respect to the conduct of the campaign.   The individual foreign officer did not suffer by it, for his associates, who were able on near inspection to judge of his intentions, did them justice. The Author, for instance, almost always had to boast of the best reception, and especially of the most friendly treatment from his comrades.

It was thus that Kutusow's arrival excited new confidence in the army ; the evil genius of the foreigners was exorcised by a true Russian, a Suwarow on a small scale, and it was not doubted that a battle would ensue without delay, which would mark the culminating point of the French offensive.

Barclay, however, had been trundled back from Witebsk to Wiasma, like one who has lost his balance, and cannot stop himself, and Kutusow could not at first succeed in recovering a fast footing for the army. He marched through Gschatsck, which, like Wiasma, was set on fire, and took up on the 3d of September a position at Borodino, which seemed to him good enough for a battle, and which he therefore set to work to fortify. This position was in fact selected by the same eyes which had chosen all the positions of Barclay—the eyes of Colonel Toll; and it was assuredly not the best among the many which that officer had thought fit for the purpose of a battle.

Kutusow, fifteen years older than Barclay, was approaching his seventieth year, and no longer in possession of the activity of mind and body, which sometimes is found in soldiers even of this age. In these respects then he was inferior to Barclay, but in natural qualities certainly superior. Kutusow had been in youth what the French call a *sabreur*, and united with this much cleverness, cunning, and dexterity. These qualities come into the composition of a good general. He had, however, lost the disastrous battle of Austerlitz against Buonaparte, and this spot had never been washed out. A situation like the present, at the head of a colossal military power, to handle several hundred thousands of men opposed to similar aggregations on immense spaces, and with the national strength of Russia confided to his care, to save or to lose that whole empire — these were conditions too expansive for his mental vision to embrace, and to which his natural endowments were not equal. The Emperor felt this, and took up again the idea of governing the whole for himself, but in this case from Petersburg, and without the assistance of so incapable an adviser as Phull.

In the centre however, at the head of the two armies of the West, Kutusow was compelled to come forward as an independent commander, and this command was one of the proudest of which history bears record, namely, the conduct of 120,000 Russians against 130,000 French with Buonaparte at their head.

In our opinion, Kutusow's discharge of this great function was anything but brilliant, and even far below the level at which his previous performances had placed him in the public expectation.

The Author was too little about the immediate person of this commander, to be able to speak with full conviction of his personal activity. He saw him for a moment only in the battle of Borodino, and had under his observation only that which immediately after that battle was the opinion of the army at large; and according to this, in the individual scenes of this great act, he was almost a nullity. He appeared destitute of inward activity, of any clear view of surrounding occurrences, of any liveliness of perception, or independence of action. He suffered the subordinate directors of the contest to take their own course, and appeared to be for the individual transactions of the day nothing but an abstract idea of a central authority. The Author admits, that in this judgment he may be in error, and that it is not the result of a searching inspection; but he never in after years has seen reason to change the idea he then formed of General Kutusow. Kutusow was then, as far as personal influence on events is concerned, a lesser agent than Barclay, which may principally be attributed to his greater age. Kutusow, nevertheless, was worth more at the head of the whole. Cunning and prudence are qualities which adhere to men even in extreme age, and they had so adhered to Kutusow; and with these he overlooked his own position and that of his adversary better than Barclay with his limited mental vision.

The result of the campaign, which at its commencement could only have been conjectured by a man of extended views, clear understanding, and rare greatness of mind, was now so near the eye as to be easily embraced by one of ordinary acuteness.

Buonaparte had involved himself in so difficult a transaction, that things began of themselves to work for the Russians, and a good result was inevitable without much exertion on their part. Kutusow would certainly not have delivered the battle of Borodino, from which he probably expected no victory, if he had not been compelled to it by the voice of the court, the army, and the nation at large. He probably looked upon it only as a necessary evil; he knew the Russians, and understood how to deal with them. With astonishing assurance he proclaimed himself the conqueror, announced every where the approaching destruction of the enemy's army, gave himself to the last moment the appearance of an intention to protect Moscow by a second battle, and suffered no device of boasting to escape him. In this fashion he flattered the vanity of the army and people; he endeavoured by proclamations and religious addresses to work on the public mind; and thus there arose a new kind of confidence, factitious indeed, but which was founded on a practical basis, the bad condition of the French army. This levity then, and this mountebankism of the old fox, was more useful at the moment than Barclay's honesty. The latter had utterly despaired of the result of the campaign, for he despaired even in October, when most men's hopes revived. He had found no resources in himself, and his anxiety had excluded those which other men could offer him, for he declared himself, for example, against the march on the Kaluga road. In his melancholy and

troubled countenance every soldier had read the
desperate condition of the state and the army; and
the voice of the commander had perhaps communicated its tone to the army, the court, and the
nation; in short, Barclay, simple-minded, honourable, personally active, but poor in ideas, and incapable of viewing profoundly the great circumstances
of the time, was overwhelmed by the moral influence of the French victory, while the more frivolous
Kutusow opposed to it vaunting and assurance,
and thus sailed with success into the gap which by
this time yawned in the line of the French armada.

When Kutusow took the command, General Yermalof was chief of the staff, and Colonel Toll
quarter-master-general to the 1st army of the West;
and inasmuch as its commander had hitherto commanded in chief, to a certain extent they held these
functions for both armies; the orders at least, which
concerned both, were issued by these officers. As
soon as Barclay receded into the mere command of
the 1st army, these two were similarly affected.
This was ostensibly the case with General Yermalof,
for with Kutusow the general of cavalry, Count
Benningsen, joined the army as chief of the staff.
It is probable that Benningsen had managed this
appointment for himself at Petersburg, well fore-
seeing that they would not give him one of the
armies, and to be in the way of the first station
should things go ill with the old general. By
degrees he asserted his claim to a certain degree of
influence, but not with the particular good-will of

the old man, who probably looked upon him with distrust. With the army this extraordinary arrangement produced an almost comic impression. The prince did not, however, bring a quarter-master-general with him to the army, and Colonel Toll held that office as before, whether actually named to it or as a locum tenens, the Author is still ignorant.

Colonel Toll had, as before, to direct the selection of positions, and the tactical dispositions connected with their choice; and thus the position of Borodino and the distribution of the troops there were for the most part his work.

Before we speak of the battle, we wish to offer some considerations on the retreat in the direction of Moscow.

The Russian army determined to retire, not upon Petersburg, but into the interior, because it could be there best reinforced and make front in all directions against the enemy. As long as the enemy was very superior in force, it was necessary to look to the protection of Moscow, since it was in his power to send a considerable force there, just as the protection of Petersburg was provided for by the detached corps of Wittgenstein. In order to avoid further weakening the army by a second detachment, it was natural for the main army to adhere to the Moscow road: could they have foreseen the rapid melting away of the French army, it would have been possible to have adopted from Smolensko the plan of quitting that direction, and choosing another road into the interior, that for example of Kaluga and Tula, since it might have been argued, that the superiority of the French being at an end, it was no longer in their power to detach a corps to Moscow, and that with their one line of connection with their base, it would still less be possible for them to pass by the Russian army on their way thither. If we also reflect that at Borodino the French were only 130,000 to 120,000, we cannot doubt that another direction of the Russian retreat, such as that of Kaluga, would have thrown Moscow out of the operations. At the periods, however, of the successive retreats from Drissa on Witebsk, and thence on Smolensko, no one entertained the idea that the French force would so soon dissolve away, the idea of clinging to the Moscow line was quite natural, in order to preserve that important place as long as possible.

At Smolensko, the relative proportions were 180,000 to 120,000, and as calculations might be erroneous, it might be considered possible that the French there had 200,000. The Russian generals then were not to be blamed, if, under these circumstances, they would not yet commit themselves to a manœuvre for the indirect defence of Moscow. Even however, if this idea had been embraced at Smolensko, it was then perhaps too late; for if, generally speaking, the alteration of a line of operation with a considerable army is much more difficult than is usually supposed, it is doubly difficult in a country like Russia, scantily peopled, for an army so considerable, and pressed by a superior force. It must always encamp, always be collected, and can therefore only subsist from magazines : these were established on the Moscow road, and would have been to be removed in the first instance; every thing in the way of ammunition, depôts, reinforcements, &c. on the Moscow road, or in march towards it, must have been thrown sideways in the new direction: whether at Smolensko there was time for all this, admits at the least of doubt.

From this it is clear that the censure which some writers have cast subsequently on the Russian generals for not having marched from Smolensko on Kaluga, is not well considered. Had they determined on this, the resolution should have been sooner adopted: they could not have adopted it sooner, because this indirect defence of Moscow did not become natural till later; and earlier would have been a theoretical hazard, which a mere general, without even full powers, could not have contemplated.

One of these writers (Buturlin) laments that General Barclay was not aware of the principle that, in war, an object is always best covered by a side position. In such a position every thing depends on the space, on the relative strength, moral as well as physical; in short, on all the elements of war. If this axiom is to hold good, its conditions must be otherwise expressed; and with such principles in view it is natural to find fault with actual results, and to see facilities where, in the execution, the path would be narrowed by difficulties.

But Barclay and his staff took no thought at the time of such a side direction, for which the colossal dimensions of the Russian empire gave such facilities. The Russian realm is so large that we may play at hide and seek in it with an enemy's army, and this fact must be the groundwork of its defence against a superior enemy. A retreat into the interior draws an enemy after it, but leaves so much territory behind him that he cannot occupy it. There is scarcely a difficulty then for the retreating army to retrace its march towards the frontier, and to reach it *pari passú* with the then weakened force of the enemy.

The side march on the Kaluga road and the retreat in this direction is something of the kind, only that things then took a more advantageous turn. No one, indeed, had previously thought on this retreat at so sharp an angle; and the idea first disclosed itself after the battle of Borodino. Such an idea, then, had not been originally spoken of among the generals and the staff; and I am not aware, that any other officers of the army had expressed it. At the moment, then, when a pressing emergency might have led to it, namely, when they began to perceive that Moscow could no longer be protected, it was already too late, since, as we have said before, the necessary preparations had not been made.

Let us now turn to the battle of Borodino. This battle is one of those which require little elucidation, since the consequences exactly corresponded to the circumstances: 120,000 Russians, of which 30,000 were Cossacks and militia, stand in a very indifferent position against 130,000 French, commanded by Buonaparte. What could be expected from such proportions, with a nearly equal balance of bravery, in such a contracted space, but what happened? namely, a slight inclination of the scale to the disadvantage of Russia. We have never been able to explain, why men so eagerly called for explanation of the battle of Borodino. The one party could not comprehend why Kutusow abandoned the field, having won the victory; the other, why Buonaparte did not annihilate the Russians.

Russia is very poor in positions. Where the great morasses prevail, the country is so wooded that one has trouble to find room for a considerable number of troops. Where the forests are thinner, as between Smolensko and Moscow, the ground is level—without any decided mountain ridges—without any deep hollows; the fields are without enclosures, therefore everywhere easy to be passed; the villages of wood, and ill adapted for defence. To this it is to be added, that even in such a country the prospect is seldom unimpeded, as small tracts of wood constantly interpose. There is therefore little choice of positions. If a commander, then, wishes to fight without loss of time, as was Kutusow's case, it is evident that he must put up with what he can get.

It was thus that Colonel Toll could find no better position than that of Borodino, which is, however, a deceptive one, for it promises at first sight more than it performs. The right wing leaning on the Moskwa, which is not fordable; the front covered by the Kolotscha, which flows in a tolerably deep valley. This is, at first sight, not so bad, and took the fancy of the quarter-master-general from the first; but the road from Smolensko to Moscow runs unfortunately not at right angles to the Kolotscha, but parallel to it for some distance, and, after it has passed the river, diverges from it at an obtuse angle near the small village of Gorki. The consequence is, if the position be taken up parallel to the stream, the army stands obliquely to its line of retreat, and exposes its left flank to the enemy. This parallel position could be the less adopted here, because, at half a mile from the great road, a second road to Moscow issues from the village of Jelnia, and thus leads straight behind the rear of such a position. Every position, moreover, at a point where, as in this case, a road makes a strong angle, is defective; for the enemy, by a simple advance, has half accomplished the turning its flank, the line of retreat is threatened from the first, and the resistance is thereby impaired. It is true the assailing party is similarly exposed; but as he is entirely prepared for advance and movement, and the enemy less so, the advantage must ordinarily accrue to the former in such an anomalous case. In this respect, therefore, the left flank was too much threatened to

allow of its being more exposed by means of a line
of retreat not perpendicular to the position. The
consequence was, that the right wing, parallel with
the Kolotscha to the right of the Moscow road, had
a very fine position, but that the centre was already
at a distance from the stream, and the left wing
was necessarily bent back *en potence*. In this way
the whole assumed the form of a convex arc; the
French attack, in consequence, was necessarily
comprehensive, and concentric in its fire; a circumstance of great moment in a narrow space and with
so vast a force of artillery. The ground taken up
by the left wing presented no particular advantages.
Some hillocks with a gentle slope, and perhaps
twenty feet high, together with strips of shrubby
wood, formed so confused an whole, that it was
difficult to pronounce which party would have the
advantage of the ground. The best side of the
position, however, the right wing, could be of no
avail to redeem the defects of the left. The whole
position too strongly indicated the left to the French
as the object of operation, to admit of their forces
being attracted to the right. It was therefore an
useless squandering of troops to occupy this portion.
It would have been far better to have let the right
wing lean on the Kolotscha itself in the neighbourhood of Gorki, and merely to have observed the
remaining ground as far as the Moskwa, or have
pretended to occupy it.

The left wing was, as we have observed, thrown
back and without support. On this account it was

fortified, and the corps of General Tutschkow reinforced by the Moscow militia. Thus a mass of some 15,000 men was stationed on the Moscow old road, so far back and so covered that it could fall on the rear and right flank of the advance itself of an enemy who intended to turn the left wing. The intention was in our opinion very good, but failed, because the force and dimensions were not in proportion to the whole, as we shall hereafter explain. The works which had been thrown up lay partly on the left wing, partly before the centre, and one of them, as an advanced post, a couple of thousand paces before the left wing. These works were only ordered at the moment when the army arrived in position. They were in a sandy soil, open behind, destitute of all external devices, and could therefore only be considered as individual features in a scheme for increasing the defensive capabilities of the position. None of them could hold out against a serious assault, and in fact most of them were lost and regained two or three times. It must, however, be said of them, that they contributed their share to the substantial and hearty resistance of the Russians; they formed for the left wing, the only local advantage which remained to the Russians in that quarter.

The Russians had in the beginning, that is, before they applied their right wing differently, about five corps of infantry in their front in two lines, the cavalry behind also in two lines, two corps with 4000 cuirassiers behind as reserve, and,

besides, the 15,000 men under Tutschkow in concealment on the left, which might also be considered
as a reserve. It may therefore be said, that they
were disposed in two lines with a third and fourth
line of cavalry behind, and a third besides of their
whole force as reserve. If we reflect, that the first
position of the Russians occupied only some 8000
paces in extent, that the five corps which formed
the first line were 40,000 strong, thus 20,000
in each line, and if we consider also the great
proportion of artillery (six pieces to 1000 men),
we shall see that the disposition was a very deep
one. If we further consider, that the corps of
Baggowut and Ostermann being found useless on
the right wing, were subsequently removed thence
and brought to the support of other points, and
were in fact used as reserves; it will be plain that
the Russian army fought on this occasion in so
confined and deep a disposition, that there is hardly
a second example of such. Equally crowded and
in similar depth was the French army drawn up,
for the greater extension of their front line, adopted
to embrace that of the enemy, was perhaps more
than compensated by their superiority in number.
This is the characteristic and main feature of the
battle, and explains,

1. The very solid and obstinate resistance of the
Russians. The battle began at six in the morning
and lasted till four P. M., and in these ten hours,
the Russians on their left wing, where they lost
most ground, gave way only to the extent of some

1500 to 2000 paces. The corps alone of Tutschkow, which entered the fray separated from the others, was driven further back. They did not, moreover, in this ten hours' struggle lose the order of their masses. Both these negative results were clearly due to the depth of their formation, for where space is afforded for cavalry rapidly to follow up the advantages gained by infantry and artillery, a partial flight must usually occur, confusion to a certain extent, and heavy losses.

2. The enormous loss of men is also explained. According to Boutourlin, the Russians lost in the two days about 50,000 men, of whom few were prisoners. In the army, the loss was rated at 30,000, which to us seems more probable; but even this, being a fourth part of the whole, is an unusual number.

Colonel Toll was fond of deep formations, *i. e.* of a small extension of front and a heavy reserve. The Author is also of this view, as considering them to afford the best means in a defence of resuming the offensive, and of depriving the assailant of the advantage of the last disposition, and thus of a surprise. He had often conversed with Colonel Toll on the subject, and it is the less doubtful to him, that the formation at Borodino was directed by that officer. We cannot, however, concur with him as to the application of his principle in this instance. In our opinion, the field of battle required more depth, *i. e.* the cavalry and reserves should have been further back. We consider the time gone by, when a battle could be treated as a single act, in which the victory could be gained at one shock, by the dexterous combination of all parts of the machine. No such time perhaps ever was, but theory has for the most part turned on this idea. The surprises by which Frederick the Great won the victories of Leuthen and Rossbach, from which the idea of his so named oblique order of battle obtained credit, were long at the bottom of this notion. If we, however, reflect how slowly all great battles progress, slowly with reference at least to the time necessary for a tactical evolution; that in fact, a consumption and wearing away of the force on each side by the fire must precede the decisive blow, which can therefore only be struck at a late hour; it seems to us unquestionable, that a reserve far to the rear, which to a certain extent has not yet appeared in the field, and which appears there, when it does so, like a newly arrived auxiliary force, can always be of effect for the decision. The advantages are,

1. That these reserves suffer nothing from the fire.

2. They can be more easily entirely concealed.

3. They can be more easily used for outflanking manœuvres.

We cannot in this place fully develope this our notion; we will only express it rather more distinctly by saying, that we have in our eye a distance of from 3000 to 4000 or 5000 paces, and must naturally admit that the local features of the ground must essentially influence the particular case, and must often render this depth of formation impossible.

In the position, however, of Borodino, where Colonel Toll shewed such deference to the principle of depth in reference to the number of lines behind each other, the other element, that of depth of ground, was too much neglected. The cavalry stood from 300 to 400 paces behind the infantry, and from these to the great reserve the distance was scarcely 1000 paces. The consequence was that both the cavalry and the reserve suffered severely from the enemy's fire without being engaged. If we recollect what masses of artillery were used in this battle by the Russians, that the Russian artillery, on account of the quantity of small ammunition carts it uses, takes up more room than any other, we may imagine how the space was filled and crammed up: the author retains to this moment the effect produced on his mind by the spectacle which the position presented in this particular.

Had the cavalry stood 1000 paces in rear of the infantry, it would have been as well and better placed for repelling any considerable success of the French. The guards, however, and General Tutschkow placed at double the above distance behind, had not suffered from the enemy's fire before they were able to open their own, and might have been employed with more sudden effect, and in every respect more usefully than they were.

The Author has dwelt thus long on the consideration of this feature in the battle of Borodino, because he esteems it a very important one in our times, because it is one which deserves attention more or less in all battles, especially in those of a defensive character, and because it distinguishes that of Borodino more than any other, the other dispositions in that action presenting in our opinion little novelty. To these, however, we now turn our attention.

Buonaparte with his united force of 130,000 men advances against the Russian position, passes with the greater part of his troops over the Kolotscha beyond the sphere of the Russian fire, and determines, as the circumstances obviously indicate, to make his principal attack on the left wing, which Poniatowski is directed to reach and to turn.

On the 5th takes place the preliminary action for the advanced fortified post in front of Bagration; the result of this was, that, after an obstinate contest, the Russians were compelled, towards evening, to abandon the work to the French, in order not to waste too much of their strength on this *hors d'œuvre*. On the 7th at 6 o'clock A. M. began the real battle. Eugene with some 40,000 men found himself on the left bank of the Kolotscha with orders to attack the Russian centre. Davoust and Ney, with about as many on the right bank, were to move against the left wing. Junot, the guards, and a part of the cavalry reserve, formed a body of 40,000 placed as reserves behind Davoust and Ney; and Poniatowski with his corps of 10,000 men was to move on the old Moscow road, and to turn the left flank. This advance of Poniatowski brought General Tutschkow into play earlier than the Russians had calculated. The action there, however, first began to be serious between 8 and 9 o'clock, after it had already lasted some hours on the other points. As Poniatowski's movement was intended for the turning the left flank, but being occupied by Tutschkow, he was unable to accomplish this purpose, we may say that the corps of the latter acted in all respects as a reserve. Poniatowski was 10,000 strong, Tutschkow 15,000, of which, however, only about half were regular troops. Poniatowski, therefore, could not master his adversary, and was ultimately strengthened by 10,000 men under Junot, whereupon Tutschkow, himself mortally wounded, was compelled to abandon the field and to retire a quarter of a mile, by which movement he reached a position which caused the Russian army uneasiness for their line of retreat.

In the centre and on the right wing the battle began at about 6 A. M., and was maintained for several hours by an heavy artillery fire, and that of the Russian jäger regiments, of which two were attached to each division, and which, generally thrown forward before the first line of their respective corps, formed a line of tirailleurs, and protected by not unimportant local obstacles, defended themselves with dexterity. It might be about 8 o'clock when the village of Borodino, on the other side of the Kolotscha and defended by a jäger regiment,

had been already taken, and the contest was going
on for the works constructed in front of the centre,
that it was determined by the Russians to make an
offensive movement on the left flank of the French.

General Platoff had been employed with some
2000 Cossacks to discover a ford of the Kolotscha
on the Russian right, had passed over, and was
astonished where he had expected to find the entire
left wing of the enemy to meet with few or no
troops.   He saw the left wing of the vice-king
moving against Borodino, and it seemed to him that
nothing would be easier than to fall on its left flank,
et cætera.   *Et cætera* we say, because it is very
usual that people do not know precisely what
they are aiming at by such a flank attack.   To go
headlong on an exposed artillery of reserve — to
capture ammunition-waggons here and there, seems
often, in prospect, of more importance than it really
is.   In short, Platoff despatched the Prince of Hesse
Philipsthal, who was with him as a volunteer, to
General Kutusow to acquaint him with the discovery he had made, and to make the proposal to
throw a considerable body of cavalry over the river
by the ford, and fall on the exposed flank of the
enemy.   The Prince of Hesse, who was perhaps
more taken with the idea. than Platoff himself,
but was a young officer without experience, betook
himself to Colonel Toll, and represented the case
with so much liveliness, that at first it really had a
winning appearance.   Colonel Toll was gained over,
and rode directly to Kutusow, who was stationed

near the village of Gorki. The Author, who at this moment was quarter-master-general to the 1st cavalry corps under Uwarow, happened to be, in the suite of that general, close to General Kutusow, when Colonel Toll rode up.

The latter had just returned from the left wing, and brought a report that all was going on favourably, P. Bagration having repulsed every attack. (In the first two hours of the action it could not well be otherwise.) At the same moment arrived an account that in the redoubt of the centre, which had for a moment been regained from the French who had stormed it, the King of Naples had been taken prisoner. The enthusiasm blazed up like lighted straw; several voices proposed to make this known to all the troops; some calmer heads among the general officers thought the fact so improbable as to require further confirmation: it was, however, believed for half an hour, although no King of Naples made his appearance, which was accounted for by the supposition of his being severely wounded. We now know that it was General Bonami, and not the King, whom the French had left, wounded, in the redoubt.

It was in this enthusiasm, and the belief of a successful turn of affairs, that the proposal of the P. of Hesse was laid before Kutusow by Colonel Toll; and it was plain that this officer, too much carried away by the pervading feeling, believed that a lively diversion with a corps of cavalry on the enemy's left would strike an effectual blow, and perhaps decide the battle. He proposed, then, to apply to this purpose the 1st cavalry corps, which consisted of 2500 horses of the light cavalry of the guard, and which, placed behind the right wing, had hitherto stood idle. Kutusow, who had been listening to all the reports and discussions like one who did not exactly know whether he stood on his head or his heels, and only from time to time said " C'est bon, faites le!" replied also to this proposal " C'est bon, prenez le!" The P. of Hesse had offered to guide the corps through the ford to the point in question. General Uwarow, therefore, was ordered to follow his guidance; and, when arrived, to fall on the enemy in flank and rear. This instruction was certainly an usual one, and the circumstances hardly admitted of more detailed orders; but, according to our experience of military matters, we could hardly consider it satisfactory. A due estimate of the magnitude of the undertaking was wanting: if it could be determined in the face of a superior enemy to give out of hand, and to abstract from the order of battle 2500 horsemen, it ought to have been capable of demonstration, that they would be of real use where they were going.

That the General Uwarow was to attack any inferior or equal cavalry force he might fall in with was in the nature of his commission; but it was easy to foresee that he would also fall in with infantry; and if his movement was to take serious effect, an infantry in force, and combined with artillery. We know however well, how it fares when a single arm is opposed to two others; General Uwarow had, it is true, twelve pieces of flying artillery with him, but this was an unimportant fraction among such masses of artillery as were used in this action: it is, then, our opinion they should have made it the duty of General Uwarow to attack whatever he met with, and have contemplated not so much a decisive advantage as a brisk attack, which would employ a considerable mass of the enemy, and withdraw it from the attack of the Russian position. Under this view even General Uwarow's ultimate failure might not have been considered as a calamity; such a commission is always disagreeable, and requires much self-denial and good-humour. It is not, however, to be expected that any general will act in this sense without specific orders; he will rather follow the common rule, seek for an equal contest, and avoid a hopeless one.

At the moment when this operation was determined on, between 8 and 9 A. M., the battle was in its first stage of development: not the least of its ultimate results could be foreseen. A long day of twelve hours was before us; and from the characteristic obstinacy of our adversary, fresh exertions were to be expected to the last moment; it was a realisation of the proverb, not to praise the day until evening has arrived. A diversion by 2500 horse could not possibly have a decisive influence on a battle delivered on one side by 130,000 men; it could at best put a spoke in the wheel of their plans for a moment, and astonish them more or less. Had this been entered upon at a moment when the decision was at hand, when exhaustion on both sides was sure to give effect to any exertion of remaining force, something might have been expected from it. At such an early hour, however, the enemy had manifestly time to gather an overwhelming force against this isolated attack, to beat General Uwarow out of the field, and return afterwards to his own business on hand.

We shall speak later of the offensive, which the Russians might have engrafted upon their defensive system, and will follow for the present General Uwarow in his enterprise.

He passed the Kolotscha by a ford above Staroie, then brought his right shoulder forward, and took a direction towards Borodino, in pursuing which, however, he was obliged, on account of some marshy rivulets which fall into the Kolotscha, to incline sensibly to the right. It was between 11 and 12 when he reached the brook which flows by Borodino into the Kolotscha. The village lay on his left, in which the troops of the vice-king had established themselves; before him was the brook, which runs through swampy meadows. On his side of it stood a couple of regiments of cavalry, and a mass of infantry, which might be a regiment or a strong battalion. The French cavalry retired immediately over a dam, which crosses the brook at about 2000 paces from Borodino; the infantry, however, was bold enough to remain, and form square with the dam in their rear. General Uwarow attacked: the Author suggested in vain that the artillery should first open upon them; the Russian officers feared that they would then retire, and escape capture. The Hussars of the Guard were therefore advanced, and ordered to charge; they made three ineffectual attacks; the infantry (Italian troops) lost neither their composure nor their ranks, and returned a steady fire. The Hussars retired, as usually happens in such cases, some thirty paces, and withdrew out of fire. General Uwarow then discontinued these not very brilliant attempts, and caused the artillery to open; at the first discharge the enemy retired over the defile. The whole affair then came to an end.

Borodino itself could not be attacked with cavalry; the brook could only be crossed by cavalry at the dam: on the other side of this were discovered on hilly ground, with much brushwood, from 4000 to 5000 infantry, in single bodies; the cavalry was behind these. In Borodino were seen some strong columns, and towards the French centre, behind the line of battle, large masses in repose, which we supposed to be of the Guard. General Platoff, with his 2000 Cossacks, was a quarter of a league to the right of Uwarow, and looking for a passage over the marshy stream.

At the time of General Uwarow's arrival, several hours of the hottest conflict had passed away; the Russians began to look on things with a

different eye from that of 8 and 9 A. M.; they
felt the whole weight of the giant now upon
them, and themselves hardly equal to the burden.
The corps of Baggowut and Ostermann, which had
been placed inactive on the right, had been applied to the support of the left and centre, and
even the Guards had sent a portion of their ranks
into the fight: the reserves thus began to be deficient, while the French Guards, some 20,000 strong,
stood motionless in heavy columns, like a thunder
cloud.   The Russians could contemplate no offensive movement other than that confided to General
Uwarow.   To that officer all eyes were now
turned; and an aide-de-camp, an officer of the
general staff, an aide-de-camp of the Emperor, rode
up in succession to see whether any thing could
possibly be done in this quarter. All rode back
with the conviction that General Uwarow could
effect nothing. It both seemed no trifling matter
to pass this brook under the fire of the enemy, and
so many troops were seen standing idle as reserves
on the other side, that it was plainly impossible for
2500 horse to affect the result of the battle by any
effort in that quarter.

The Author thanked God that he had become
a nullity on this occasion, and was unable to take
part in the discussions which passed between
General Uwarow and the officers despatched to
him. He was, from the beginning, convinced that
this diversion could produce no result, and saw
now plainly that if any thing was to be made of it,

some young fire-eater, who had his reputation to make, would have been the man for the service, and not General Uwarow.

During these deliberations, which occupied some hours, there suddenly arose a heavy fire beyond the stream, out of the brushwood, upon the left wing of the French; and the account was soon spread that Platoff had at length found a passage, and with his Cossacks was in the wood on that side. We saw, in fact, these troops so remarkable for wonderful transitions from the extreme of timidity to that of daring, careering about among the masses of infantry, without making any decided attack, as if skirmishing. The troops immediately in our front feared to be locked in the morass, and made a side movement. The Cossack regiment of the Guard attached to Uwarow's corps could stand it no longer: like a rocket with its tail, they were over the dam like lightning, and into the wood to join their brethren.

Uwarow unquestionably might have followed at this moment, but he had no desire to let himself be squashed in the defile, if repulsed, or to have to make an excentrical retreat *en debandade,* as the Cossacks are accustomed to do on occasion. Having also despatched messengers in all directions to Kutusow, Benningsen, and Barclay, he remained, waiting for further orders. Before long the Cossacks of the Guard returned, and with a considerable deficit in killed and wounded. In this position we looked at the battle; and we have still in our recollection the character of weariness and exhaustion which it assumed. The infantry masses were so reduced, that, perhaps, not more than a third of their original strength was engaged. The rest were either killed, wounded, engaged in removing the wounded, or rallying in the rear. Large vacancies were every where apparent. That enormous artillery, which had brought on the two sides nearly 2000 pieces into the field, was now heard only in single shots, and even these seemed to have lost the force and thunder of their original voice, and to give a hoarse and hollow tone. The cavalry had almost every where taken up the place and position of the infantry, and made its attacks in a weary trot; riding hither and thither, disputing and gaining by turns the field works.

Towards 3 P.M. it was evident that the battle was on its last legs, and that, according to all rule, the decision depended entirely on the possession of the last trump card, i. e. the strongest reserve. This, as well as the real relative position of the two parties, we could not bring under our observation. The individual reports which reached us were not positively alarming; which the Author is now the more surprised at, because the centre had evidently already given way to some extent, from which an inference might be drawn as to the state of things on the left.

At about 3 P.M. General Uwarow received orders to retire, and take up his original position; we marched off therefore, and between 4 and 5 o'clock arrived in the rear of Gorki, and formed there.

The events of the battle had been very simple. As Tutschkow had prevented the turning of the left wing, the French pressed perpendicularly the centre and the left wing with the weight of their masses.   The left wing was strengthened after the first hour of the action by Baggowut, the centre somewhat later by Ostermann, and some detachments from the Guards were applied to the support of the front.   The battle thus maintained itself with a tremendous fire, and a reeling to and fro of single attacks, till towards 4 o'clock, when the French superiority in numbers, and also certainly in fighting skill, showed itself in some concession of ground by the Russians, the surrender of some of their works, and their withdrawal to a position in which their force was more pressed together, and the left wing pushed further back, so that it was now parallel with the road of retreat, and not above 2000 paces distant from it; while the old road was as good as in the hands of the French.

Although in the army it was thought a duty still to entertain doubt as to the result, although much was said of the necessity of maintaining the field of battle, which was not, strictly speaking, yet lost, and of winning the battle by perseverance, and by the exhaustion of the French, the affair was, in fact, fully decided, and the crafty Kutusow was in no doubt as to what course he was now compelled to adopt.   The superiority of the French, which was very observable before the battle, had only increased, for the Russian loss had been the greater.

In the ten hours' struggle the balance had not remained perfectly even, but the Russian scale had
been perceptibly depressed. No improvement could
be expected from a renewal of the action. The
position was broken in upon, the line of retreat
threatened, and the next incident in the progress
of calamity would have been a total defeat. The
army was as yet still in order, and could draw off
without losing it. Kutusow determined to commence a retreat in the night, and in this he unquestionably followed the dictates of prudence.

Buonaparte, on the other hand, could wait for
Kutusow's retreat: had his expectation of it been
defeated, and had Kutusow remained on the field
on the 8th, he must certainly have attacked him
again; and it cannot be doubted that he would have
done so. It is another question whether Buonaparte, who had time and fresh troops sufficient,
should not have made greater exertions on the
7th, and have raised his success to the pitch of a
complete victory. Such a proceeding would have
been assuredly more in the spirit of his former
performances, to which he owed such great results.
By renewed attacks with troops of all arms, he
might, perhaps, have reaped further advantages,
and attained that point where the mass of the
cavalry launched in pursuit might have achieved
the complete destruction of the enemy. If, however, we consider the situation of Buonaparte at
the moment, the extent of his whole undertaking,
the force he had devoted to it, and the consump-

tion, rapid beyond all expectation, of that force up to this period, which led him now to doubt its accomplishment, we can comprehend that the main object should now appear to him to be the preservation of his army to the period when terms of peace could be brought into discussion. He had the victory, he had good hope of entering Moscow: to improve these advantages, with some hazard to his ultimate object, seemed to him neither necessary nor wise.

We must not conclude that, in virtue of the ordinary polarity of interests of rival commanders, the one must in this instance have committed an error, and that because a renewal of the action was not in the interest of Kutusow, it was necessarily in that of his adversary. The polarity concerns the ends and not the means. Both commanders might have a common interest in seeking or in avoiding a battle. Had Buonaparte been quite certain of destroying his adversary, he would assuredly have devoted a portion of his remaining strength to that object; but the Russians are very brave: they were still in good order; the neighbouring ground, though even for Russia it might be called open, was yet not sufficiently so to be called positively favourable for cavalry. The road to Moscow is so wide, that the Russians could march on it in two columns, and yet bring off their artillery besides; thus, in fact, they could move in four columns on the same road, which greatly secured and lightened the retreat: all this promised no child's play and heavy losses. We must also further remember, that two commanders have different circles of observation, that each knows his own position better than that of the other, and that their conclusions may vary.

We confess that we see nothing to be surprised at in the results of the battle, and nothing but a natural course of events.

A few words now on the dispositions on either side.

Both sides, as we have remarked perhaps too often, were much crowded together. The flanking movement of Poniatowski was, in fact, as he had no more than 10,000 men, a little measure, which could have no real effect, and on which Buonaparte appears not much to have relied. His attack, then, was peculiarly a perpendicular impingement or pressure upon the enemy's position; but as this position was convex, the pressure was concentric, and thence some of the objects were realised, which are usually connected with an outflanking operation. That Buonaparte adhered to this simple form is a proof that he did not undervalue the probable resistance, for the simpler form is essentially the most circumspect, the least adventurous, but certainly the least decisive. Had he only amused the centre, which in respect of the ground was immeasurably stronger than the left wing, and endeavoured to outflank the left with 50,000 men instead of with 10,000, the battle would have been sooner decided, and probably greater results obtained. This form of attack was doubtless the more hazardous, because it thrust the mass of his forces further beside the line of retreat, and would have increased the difficulty in case of disaster.

Kutusow should have confessed to himself, that he had no sound reason to expect a victory over an enemy morally and physically superior. It was his business to profit by the advantages he possessed — knowledge and possession of the ground, — to act by surprise; that is, to combine the means for a powerful offensive with his defensive measures.

If this offensive was to operate by a sudden blow, the convexity of the army made it necessary that this should be organised on the flank which had to expect the enemy's attack. This was, doubtless, the left; and it was one of the advantages of the Russian position, that this could be foreseen with certainty.

We think, therefore, that Kutusow should by all means have made preparations for the defence of the ground to the right of the Moscow road as far as the Moskwa; should have made them as ostentatiously as possible, and thrown up many works; but should have occupied this part of the position only for appearance, and for the first attack; that with the remaining troops of the right wing, with General Tutschkow and a part of the cavalry of the centre and left wing, he should have formed a mass of 50,000 men, and have placed these in ambuscade, a good half league, or somewhat further, behind the left wing of the army, an operation favoured by the

prevalence of brushwood in that quarter. The
Guards would then have remained in their position
as a reserve to the defensive portion of the army,
and for the protection of the left flank against the
first burst of the enemy upon it.

Should this offensive force be set in motion after
the preliminary proceedings, that is, after some
hours of the battle had elapsed against the enemy's
right wing, the results which might be expected to
occur over and above the natural results of its
relative weight, would depend on the degree of
surprise which would attend its descent, and upon
other incidental circumstances.   In any case, however, its natural share in the action could neither
be taken away nor shortened.   The question, who
was to give way, might still have to be decided by
the preponderance of force; but the Russians must
have retained the advantage of finding themselves
on the flank of the enemy.

The Russians retired in the night of the 7th,
and, as we have said, in four contiguous and
parallel columns on one and the same road.   They
made only a mile of distance, to behind Mojaisk;
which sufficiently proves that they were in a state
of order and preparation, which is not usual after
the loss of a battle.   The Author can also attest
that there was no symptom of that dissolution
which has been attributed to it by an otherwise
very impartial writer (the Marquis de Chambray).
The number of prisoners may have reached a few
thousands; that of guns abandoned, between thirty

and forty. The trophies of victory were, therefore, trifling.

Thenceforward the retreat to Moscow was continuous, but by very easy marches. Borodino is fifteen miles from Moscow, and these were accomplished in seven marches; for on the 14th the army passed through the city.

The rear guard was confided to General Miloradowitsch, and consisted of 10,000 infantry and about as many cavalry. General Uwarow with his corps formed part of the latter. The French did not press it strongly. Murat, with a great mass of cavalry, formed the advanced guard. The two parties touched on each other usually about the afternoon, marched towards each other, skirmished and cannonaded for some hours, when the Russians retired a slight distance, and both sides formed their camp. This march had the character of weariness and strategic disability on both sides.

One day alone was an exception. On the 10th of September Miloradowitsch found himself only half a mile distant from the army, when the French made their appearance, an hour before sunset, with troops of all arms. He could not give way unless the army was to give up its intended quarters for the night; and as the ground was pretty favourable, he determined to allow the affair to come to extremities. The Russian infantry in some low wood defended itself with spirit. They occupied a small ridge, and even when driven from this fought for an hour in a situation of great disadvantage. The attacks of the French, although intended to be serious, had here also an appearance of debility. The action lasted till eleven at night, and Miloradowitsch maintained himself close behind his field of battle.

The direction of Kutusow's retreat from Mojaisk to Moscow has been made matter of censure. He might, it has been said, have pursued the road by Wereja to Tula.

On this road, however, he would not have found a morsel of bread. Every thing which an army should have in its rear, every element of its life was on the Moscow road. The Wereja road also, being in a sideward direction, was more exposed, the road-way was less convenient, the connection with Moscow ceased to be easy and direct; all these were difficulties which, in the case of a beaten army, deserved double regard. This march, however, towards Kaluga would have hardly fulfilled its own views. Moscow was now but fourteen miles distant; Buonaparte would not have hesitated to send there a corps of 30,000 men, which, under existing circumstances, he could have done with safety. Moscow would then have fallen, and Kutusow would have been accused by the shortsighted Russians of having by his scientific march surrendered the city without necessity. Kutusow adhered to his natural line of retreat, as all other commanders would probably have done in his place.

We have here one or two general observations to make on the Russian retreat and French pursuit,

which may contribute to the better understanding
of the result of the campaign. The Russians found
from Witebsk to Moscow in all the chief provincial
towns magazines of flour, grits, biscuit, and meat;
in addition to these, enormous caravans arrived
from the interior with provisions, shoes, leather,
and other necessaries: they had also at their command a mass of carriages, the teams of which were
subsisted without difficulty, since corn and oats
were on the ground, and the caravans of the country
are accustomed, even in time of peace, to pasture
their draft cattle in the meadows. This put the
Russians in condition every where to encamp where
it suited them in other respects; the chief concern
was water. The summer was unusually hot and
dry, the seat of war was not rich in water, the
smaller streams were for the most part dried up,
and we all know how little the village wells can
supply in such cases. There was, therefore, a general
want of water, and Colonel Toll thought himself
lucky when he could mark out an encampment near
a small lake.

As, with the exception of the halt at Smolensko,
the retreat from Witebsk to Moscow was in fact an
uninterrupted movement, and from Smolensko the
point of direction lay always tolerably straight to
the rear, the entire retreat was a very simple operation, which partook very little of manœuvre, and in
which no attempt of the enemy at manœuvre was
much to be feared. When an army always gives
way and retires continually in a direct line, it is

very difficult for the pursuer to outflank it or press it away from its course: in this instance, also, the roads are few, and ravines rare; the seat of war, therefore, admitted of few geographical combinations.

Every soldier must know from experience that in a retreat this simplicity greatly economises the powers of men and horses. Here were no long arranged rendezvous, no marches to and fro, no long circuits, no alarms; in short, little or no outlay of tactical skill and expenditure of strength. Even the outpost service cost the regular forces little trouble, as this duty was usually performed by the Cossacks.

Where the propinquity of two roads afforded facilities, the army marched in more than one column; where the side roads were difficult, the main force remained on the main road, a very wide one, as it was unnecessary to divide the column on the score of subsistence. It halted where most convenient, established itself as well as possible, and neither man nor horse experienced any want of subsistence; the former, indeed, went generally without bread, and had to content himself with bad biscuit, which was, however, not unwholesome, and scarcely less nourishing than bread ; grits, meat, and brandy, were in abundance; the horses seldom had corn, but Russian horses are accustomed to live upon hay, and the Author for the first time here observed that this food is more nourishing than is usually imagined. Hay was plentiful and good; the Russians give their horses from 15 to 20 lbs. a day, and they rejected the sheaves of ripe oats which lay on the fields, thinking them less wholesome.

The cavalry of the rear-guard alone (and this, indeed, was the greater number) was worse off, because it could seldom unsaddle. The Author scarcely remembers to have seen through the whole retreat a light cavalry regiment unsaddled; almost all the horses were galled.

We may gather from this that in physical respects the Russian army was well off in its ten weeks of retreat. It only suffered diminution from casualties in action, and lost few by sick or stragglers. This was apparent in the result.

Barclay and Bagration, after Wittgenstein had been detached, were at first 110,000 strong, without Cossacks. The reinforcements which joined in the retreat might amount to some 30,000 men. They marched through Moscow about 70,000 men. The loss, therefore, had been 70,000; of whom it is easy to see that the greater part is to be laid to the account of fighting casualties.

It was the reverse with the French. Just in proportion as the Russians, by extraordinary circumstances, were unusually well off in physical condition, and to a degree which could hardly have obtained in a better cultivated country, were the French involved in unusual difficulty.

The subsistence of an advancing and pursuing army is always matter of difficulty, inasmuch as before the magazines are collected, the army has always moved on a little, and a mass of carriages becomes necessary. These difficulties increase as population and culture decrease. The advancing army has but two resources for relief. It now and then captures a magazine of the enemy, and is not obliged to keep together in large masses in the same degree; can divide itself more, and live better on the inhabitants. In Russia, these resources failed; the first, because the Russians generally set fire, not only to the magazines, but to the towns and villages they abandoned; the second, by reason of the scantiness of population, and the want of side roads. In order to avail himself to some degree of the second resource, Buonaparte marched his army always in three columns, of which those to the right and left of the main road consisted usually each of one corps, *i. e.* of some 30,000 or 40,000 men. These side columns, however, had, as we learn in detail from some of the French writers, such difficulties to contend with, that they generally reached their camp late at night, and at an enormous and useless outlay (*faux frais*) of exertion.

The difficulty of subsistence, therefore, showed itself, of necessity, very early, and this fact is notorious.

The cavalry also suffered great privation. The Russians. had usually swept the adjoining fields. The French, therefore, had to forage at a distance for scanty returns.

Water was a main difficulty. The Russian rear-guard itself usually found the wells exhausted, and the smaller streams not fit to be used, and was thus driven to look out for rivers or small lakes. As, however, they could send onward and explore the country at their convenience, the evil was not so great as with the French advanced guard, which could not despatch explorers, and was obliged, in regular course, to take up a position touching on the Russian rear. There is, besides, no detailed map of the country other than that called the Podoroschna map, which the French had translated and increased in scale; on which, however, from the small scale of the original, many places of some consequence, and still more smaller objects, were wanting.

The Author has strongly in his recollection the suffering from want of water in this campaign. He never endured such thirst elsewhere. The filthiest puddles were had recourse to to quench the fever, and for a week together washing was often out of the question. How this must have affected the cavalry may be imagined, and the French, as we have remarked, must have suffered doubly. It is well known in how wretched a condition the French cavalry reached Moscow.

It was the custom with the Russian rear-guard to burn every village as they abandoned it. The inhabitants were generally withdrawn beforehand; what they contained in forage and subsistence was rapidly used, and nothing therefore remained but

the wooden houses, which in this country are of
small value.   Little reluctance therefore attended
their destruction, and little care was taken to prevent it.   What at first was carelessness and neglect,
became deliberate practice, which extended itself
widely to the towns, great as well as small.

The bridges were also destroyed, and the numbers cut away from the werst posts, which deprived
the enemy of very essential means for ascertaining
their position.   It was often difficult for the French
to know on what point of the road they stood, and
they seldom met with inhabitants to question.

By these difficulties, the French advance was
delayed, embarrassed, and made exhausting to man
and horse.   They were 12 weeks on their march
from Kauen to Moscow, a distance of 115 miles,
and out of more than 280,000 men, no more than
90,000 reached that capital.

On the 14th September, the Russian army
marched through Moscow, and the rear-guard received orders to follow on the same day; but General Miloradowitsch was also entrusted to conclude
an agreement with the King of Naples, by which
some hours should be granted to the Russian army
for the complete evacuation of the city, and ordered
to threaten, in case of refusal, an obstinate defence
at the gates and in the streets.

General Miloradowitsch sent a flag of truce to
the outposts with a request for an interview with
the King of Naples, of whom it was known that
he commanded the advanced guard.   After a few

hours it was replied that General Sebastiani was at the outposts. General Miloradowitsch was not satisfied, but nevertheless acceded, and a pretty long conference ensued, to which we of the suite were not admitted. Hereupon the two rode together a good portion of the way towards Moscow, and from their conversation the Author saw that the proposal of General Miloradowitsch had met with no difficulty. To some expressions of that officer relative to the sparing of the city as far as possible, General Sebastiani replied with the utmost eagerness, " Monsieur, l'Empereur mettra sa garde à la tête de son armée, pour rendre toute espèce de désordre impossible," &c. This assurance was several times repeated. It was remarked by the Author as expressing a strong desire for the possession of Moscow in a complete state; and, on the other hand, the request of General Miloradowitsch was such as to militate against the notion of a Russian plan for its conflagration.

Moscow had nearly the appearance of a deserted city. Some two hundred of the lowest class came to meet General Miloradowitsch, and to implore his protection. In the streets some scattered groups were seen who contemplated our march with sorrowful countenances. The streets were also so thronged with the carriages of fugitives, that the General was obliged to send forward two cavalry regiments to make room. The most painful spectacle was that of the wounded, who lay in long rows near the houses, and had hoped to have been transported with the army. These wretched beings probably all perished.

We struck, in passing through the city, on the road to Riazan, and took a position some 1000 paces behind it.

General Sebastiani had promised that the head of his advanced guard should not enter the city sooner than two hours after our departure. General Miloradowitsch was therefore much surprised, having hardly taken up his position behind the city, to see two regiments of the enemy's light cavalry deploy before us. He sent immediately a flag of truce, and demanded a conference with the King of Naples. This time, however, also, the king declined to appear, considering it perhaps beneath his dignity; and General Miloradowitsch was obliged again to content himself with General Sebastiani. He made the liveliest remonstrances against the too great rapidity of the pursuit, which admitted of easy reply, as from various causes we had taken much longer time to defile than the French had anticipated. The conference, however, led to the result that the two parties stood close opposite each other without coming to blows We saw from this position how Moscow gradually emptied itself through the gates on either side by an uninterrupted stream of the light waggons of the country, without for the first several hours being interrupted by the French. The Cossacks seemed rather to be yet in entire possession of these portions of the city, and the French advanced guard to occupy itself solely with the rear-guard of the Russians.   We saw also from where we stood wreaths of smoke rising from several places in the furthest suburbs, which, in the Author's opinion, were results of the confusion there prevailing.

The Author had the painful satisfaction, during the second interview between Miloradowitsch and Kutusow, to hear, as the two first Uhlan regiments deployed, the word of command given in German, and even with the pure Berlin accent; and they turned out, in truth, to be two Prussian regiments, one of which, the Uhlans of Brandenburgh, had been raised in Berlin.   The Author profited by this occasion to forward intelligence of himself to his friends.

As we defiled through Moscow, the Author was in the most curious expectation as to which road we should adopt.   General Uwarow was unwell: his cavalry corps was transferred to the command of Miloradowitsch; and the Author found himself in the suite of this general as a subordinate on the staff, and the orders for the direction of the retreat had by chance not been imparted to him.   He was agreeably surprised to observe, that at least that direction was not in the straight line towards Wladimir, but to the right towards Riazan.   This tallied with what had fallen in conversation at head quarters from officers of the general staff.   After the battle of Borodino, Colonel Toll had twice assured the Author, when the latter had been sent to him on business, that in his opinion the retreat beyond

Moscow could not be continued in its former direction, but must be turned southwards. The Author warmly assented, and made use of the expression, become habitual to him, that in Russia one may play at hide and seek with an enemy, and that by continually retiring one may in the end find one's self with him again on the frontier. This idea, which the Author applied jestingly in the warmth and freedom of conversation, adverted to the element of space, and to the advantage of those enormous dimensions which make it impossible for the invader to cover and occupy strategically the territory in his rear by his mere advance.

The pursuit of this idea had earlier convinced the Author that it is impossible to obtain possession of a great country with European civilisation otherwise than by aid of internal division. This form of the conception, however, was less natural to Colonel Toll, and he dwelt chiefly on the greater fertility of the southern provinces; the easier recruiting of the army; and the facility for strategical operations on the flank of the enemy. He communicated, however, to the Author his doubts as to his success in persuading others, and his fears that the conception was unpalatable to the generality.

Even the younger officers of the staff frequently discussed this idea, so that if not thoroughly illustrated, it was at least much talked over.

We mention all this to show that the march on Kaluga, which has since made so much noise in the world, and is become a sort of luminous point in the region of military speculations, in its conception and discovery, did not start suddenly from the head of commander or adviser, like a Minerva from that of Jupiter. It has become our general conviction, that ideas in war are generally so simple, and lie so near the surface, that the merit of their invention can seldom substantiate the talent of the commander who adopts them. Among five or six ideas which suggest themselves, the ability to choose the most promising, the acuteness which can pierce a cloud of obscure relations, and by the application of the judgment can decide among them on the instant, these may more properly be considered the cardinal virtues of a commander, but are something very different from mere invention.

The chief thing, however, is the relative difficulty of the execution. In war all is simple; but the most simple is still very difficult. The instrument of war resembles a machine with prodigious friction, which cannot, as in ordinary mechanics, be adjusted at pleasure, but is ever in contact with a host of chances. War is, moreover, a movement through a dense medium. A motion easy in the air is difficult in water. Toil and danger are the elements in which the mind has to act in war, and of these elements we know nothing in the closet. It thus falls out that we remain behind the line we have drawn by anticipation, and that no common powers are required to maintain us even at a medium point.

After this avowal, we think it no derogation from

the merit of the Russian commander to maintain that this notion of an oblique retreat had in itself no singular merit, and has been overrated by authors.

To put every thing in its right place, we must assert that the result of the campaign by no means emanated from this idea, or was practically dependent upon it. The altered direction of the retreat had merit principally, only if it could be considered as one of the causes of bringing the enemy out of the country. This, however, was not the case, since the French found themselves in a condition which compelled them in any case to evacuate the country, provided peace were refused. We now know enough to be sure that if Kutusow had retired on Wladimir, Buonaparte could neither have followed him there, nor have wintered in Moscow. In any case he must have retired, for he was in a strategical consumption, and required the last strength of his weakened frame to drag himself back. This we remark only to show the real connexion of causes and effects; for the march had merit in this respect, that the Russian commanders did not accurately know the condition of the enemy, and considered him capable of continuing the offensive. The flanking position of Kutusow had also the advantage of more easily operating on the enemy's line of retreat, and thus contributed something to the result, only it cannot at all be considered as the main cause of that result.

In what manner Colonel Toll prevailed in his

view is not known to the Author. The account given by Colonel Buturlin, in his history of the campaign may be true in main particulars, but we cannot easily persuade ourselves that Kutusow, when he selected the Riazan road, already contemplated his after march on that of Kaluga. He might have executed the latter more conveniently from Moscow at once, and this flank march, how well soever devised, and successful in its result, must have always appeared hazardous in previous contemplation.

That Colonel Toll, before reaching Moscow, wished to bend off towards Kaluga, was, in fact, only with the idea of not exposing Moscow to danger; for, otherwise, the deflection was easier to execute at Moscow than any where else. Kutusow chose the Riazan road because it was a middle road, in a certain degree a middle term between conflicting military opinions. It is probable that Colonel Toll was able only at a later period to persuade him to his movement to the left, because it then became apparent that it might be executed without difficulty. The French were, in fact, so occupied at first with taking possession of Moscow that they only pursued slowly, and on the Riazan road. By means of the Cossacks, who swarmed in every direction, it was known that the Podolsk road was still entirely free; that road was otherwise only covered in some degree by the Pachra, which flows in a tolerably deep valley.

On the third day after our departure from

Moscow, the 16th September, was the flank march determined upon, and executed on the 17th and 18th, whereby we came on the Tula road. It is probable that this was at first the object of the movement, and that only when the old man saw that the transaction was so well accomplished was he persuaded to the third march, that on the old Kaluga road, for we remained halted for a day on that of Tula.

The march succeeded so completely, that the French lost us entirely out of their sight for several days.

On this march we saw Moscow burning without interruption, and although we were seven miles distant, the wind sometimes blew the ashes upon us. Even though the Russians were already, by the burning of Smolensko and other towns, broken in to sacrifices of this description, yet this one filled them with real sorrow, and incensed them against the enemy, to whom they attributed this as a real act of barbarity, an effect of his hate, his insolence, and his cruelty.

This leads us to the question of the origin of the fire. The reader will have remarked that the chiefs of the army displayed to the world rather an anxiety for the preservation of Moscow, than any indication of a design for its destruction; and this was probably real. In the army, the conflagration at the moment was looked upon as a great misfortune, a real calamity. Rostopchin, whom the Author had occasion often to meet in a small circle some eight days after the event, moved heaven and earth to repudiate the idea of his being the incendiary of Moscow, an idea which arose at that time. The impression of all this, the confusion which the Author had witnessed in the streets as the rearguard defiled; the circumstance that the smoke was first seen to rise from the extremities of the suburbs still haunted by the Cossacks, conveyed to the Author's mind the conviction that the fire of Moscow was a consequence of the disorder, and of the habit into which the Cossacks had fallen of first thoroughly pillaging, and then setting on fire, every abode which they were obliged to evacuate to the enemy. That the French were not the agents he was firmly convinced, for he had seen what value they placed upon the possession of it uninjured; that the Russian authorities had done the act, appeared to him at the least not proved by any single fact, and the most eager and solemn assurances of the individual held up as the principal agent, seemed to leave no room for doubt. Had Rostopchin so acted in the sense of a great and necessary sacrifice, he would not have solemnly disclaimed it. The Author, therefore, was long unable to persuade himself that the conflagration of Moscow was a deliberate act. Subsequently, however, to what has since been said, and especially to the very unsatisfactory printed defence of Rostopchin, he not only became doubtful in his opinion, but he almost arrived at the conviction that Rostopchin certainly set it on fire, and this on his own responsibility, without foreknowledge of the government. Perhaps his long disgrace, his long absence from Russia, were the consequences of such an assumption of power, which a Russian autocrat seldom forgives.

The government had probably only contemplated the evacuation of the city, the removal of all the authorities, and of the inhabitants of the better classes; if, indeed, the government had time for interposition at all, which is only conceivable on the supposition that it contemplated the evacuation from the time when Smolensko was abandoned. In any case this particular measure, if emanating from Rostopchin alone, would have had its approval. From such a measure as this to incendiarism is certainly a step. It is not probable that the government, that is, the Emperor, should have willed it. It resembles too little his feeble character, and as little is it appropriate to a ministry, which is an isolated machine, and not liable to the enthusiastic impulses, or the fanaticism of a great popular assembly. On the other hand, the responsibility assumed by Rostopchin was enormous, since in the end, however simple the execution, he must have employed agents, who must have received orders from his mouth. If he was really the author, we can come to no other conclusion, than that the state of passion and bitterness, in which he certainly appeared at the time, lent him the energy for the action, for the execution of which he could expect neither thanks nor honours.

The personal character of the man was not such as to leave ground for the supposition, that an enthusiastic temperament or mere fanaticism were with him the main spring of the transaction. He possessed the manners and the polish of a man of the world, grafted on a strong Russian stock. He was on terms of decided hostility with Kutusow, and loudly assailed him for the impudent falsehood with which to the last moment he led the world to believe that he would venture on a second battle for the salvation of Moscow.

In any case it is one of the most remarkable phenomena in history, that an action which in public opinion had so vast an influence on the fate of Russia should stand out like the offspring of an illegitimate amour, without a father to acknowledge it, and to all appearance should be destined to remain wrapt in eternal mystery.

That the conflagration was a great misfortune for the French is certainly not to be denied : it alienated the Emperor's mind further from all idea of negotiation, and was a means for exalting the national spirit—and these were its principal evils for the French. It is, however, an exaggeration to say, with most of the French, that it was the main cause of their failure. Many objects of necessity were doubtless destroyed, of which they might have availed themselves; but the indispensable was men, and these Moscow, however preserved, could not have supplied.

An army of 90,000 men, with exhausted troops

and ruined horses, the end of a wedge driven 120 miles into Russia, an army of 110,000 men on their right, an armed people around them, compelled to show a front to all points of the compass, without magazines, with insufficient ammunition, with but one, entirely devastated, line of communication with its base—this is not a situation to pass a winter in.   If, however, Buonaparte was not certain of maintaining himself through the winter in Moscow, it became necessary for him then to commence his retreat before the winter set in, and the preservation or the reverse of Moscow could have no immediate influence on his plans.   His retreat was unavoidable, and his whole campaign a failure, from the moment that the Emperor Alexander refused him peace: every thing was calculated on this peace, and Buonaparte assuredly never for a moment deceived himself on this point.

We purpose to make an observation or two at the close of our narrative on his plan of campaign, and we postpone till then our further remarks.

In the Russian army there prevailed at this time a condition of grief and despondency, which led men to consider an early peace as the sole resource. Not that the army itself was without courage: among the soldiers there was rather a feeling of pride and superiority, which, justifiable or not, had still a powerful influence; but there was little confidence in the general direction of affairs, the feeling of the immense losses already incurred by the state seemed overwhelming, and any distinguished firmness and energy on the part of the government, appeared not to be expected. This made peace not only expected, but desired. How P. Kutusow was inclined, no one ever rightly knew: he assumed, however, the appearance of determined opposition to all negotiation.

We gather from this, how imperfectly the scope of this great transaction was embraced by the army. We nevertheless touched upon the culminating point of the French offensive, the point where the whole weight of the burthen should be rolled back upon him who had raised it. General Barclay, who held the second place in the army, and, as war minister, was necessarily most intimately entrusted with the whole war, said near Woronowo early in October, some fourteen days therefore before the French retreat, to the author and some other officers who presented themselves to him on their transference to some distant appointments, " Thank your God, gentlemen, that you are called away from hence; no good can come out of this history."

We were of a different opinion; but then we were foreigners, and it was easier for us, as such, to look at things without prejudice. How great soever was our sympathy, we were not, like Russians, immediately involved in the agonies of a country of our own, wounded, suffering, and threatened in its very existence. Such feelings must influence the judgment. We trembled only at the thought of a peace, and saw, in the calamities of the moment, the means of salvation. We sup-

pressed, however, any open declaration of senti-
ments which would have made us looked upon
with doubtful countenances.

In Petersburgh the turn of affairs was accurately
judged of, and to the honour of the Emperor we
must say, not only in the last moment, but at an
earlier period of events.

The circumstantial reports which the Emperor
received from the army of the daily losses of the
enemy, and which were perhaps forwarded more as
anodynes than under a positive conviction of their
truth; the victory of Wittgenstein at Kliastitzi;
the first battle of Polotsk, where victory remained
uncertain in despite of the French superiority; the
capture of the Saxon corps at Kobrin; the approach
of the army of Moldavia on the one wing, and that
of Steinheil on the other; the long retreat into the
interior to beyond Smolensko, albeit rather the
result of circumstances than of premeditation; all
this had unfolded a dawning of hope to those in
Petersburgh. Removed as they were an hundred
miles from the fields of blood, the devastated towns
and villages, the spectacle of painful retreat and
triumphant pursuit, their judgments were calmer
and firmer. In this point of view the Emperor's
departure from the army is to be considered as a
piece of great good fortune.

In Petersburgh, then, animated by the first indications of the possibility of a favourable result, fortified by the advice of some men of energy, among
whom the Baron von Stein is certainly to be reck-

oned, the Emperor embraced the resolution to listen to no offers of peace, to push forward to the utmost preparations for war on every point, and to conduct the course of it himself, in its leading features, from Petersburgh.

We have seen that the idea of falling back in the centre, and operating on the two flanks of the enemy had been the original conception of the campaign, though on a very reduced scale. Circumstances had now so shaped themselves that the centre was deep in Russia, while the right wing of the French was still on the frontier, and the left on the Dwina. The two main reinforcements to Russia of regular troops, the Moldavian army and that of Finland, had their own natural direction against the wings; it was therefore natural, but not the less meritorious in the Emperor, that he determined to revert to the first idea, but to carry it out on a larger scale. It was therefore resolved to bring into operation two armies in South Lithuania and two in north in the rear of the grand French army, namely, Tschitschagow, Sacken, Wittgenstein, and Steinheil, which were intended to overpower the inferior forces in their respective fronts, and then to advance on the great line of French communication with the centre, to cut the thread of its strategic existence, and to waylay the French retreat.

This resolution was adopted early in September at Petersburgh, and the necessary dispositions adopted. The result of Borodino was not then known. It is plain, however, that the arrangement was calculated more on the supposition of a defeat than a victory, and this was prudent. Up to this point the conduct of the Emperor deserves the highest praise. It was, however, unpractical, and savouring of inexperience in war, that these dispositions for the four armies were much too circumstantially framed. The result proves this, for not one of them could be executed. It is remarkable, and illustrative of Russian administration, that the forces which were to be placed in Riga and under Wittgenstein never reached the half of the numbers stated at Petersburgh. These facts, taken together, give a ludicrous effect to a comparative perusal of the orders issued at Petersburgh, and the record of what occurred. Colonel Michaud of the general staff, aide-de-camp to the Emperor, was supposed to have had a principal share in framing these dispositions. He was an officer of much instruction, from the Piedmontese service, who knew however little of the conduct of war on a great scale, was not clear in his conceptions, nor practical in their execution.

Immediately after the evacuation of Moscow, the General Miloradowitsch gave up the command of the rear-guard, which was transferred to General Rajefsky. The composition also of the rear-guard was altered, and this gave to the Author occasion to attend at head-quarters, as disposable for other service. On announcing himself to General Benningsen, he found an order from the Emperor, by which he was appointed chief of the general staff to the garrison of Riga. That post had been filled by another officer from the Prussian service, a Lieutenant Colonel von Tiedemann, who had fallen in the sally of the 22d of August. The Emperor thought it expedient to have a German officer there, and the Author occurred to him. The order had lain for some weeks at head-quarters, and in the confusion of daily occurrences would have been quite overlooked, if a younger officer had not kindly informed the Author of its existence.

To be attached to General Essen certainly promised him a more agreeable sphere of activity than a post with a division or cavalry corps of the main army; where, from ignorance of the language, he could only by the greatest efforts perform the commonest duties. The campaign from this cause had been doubly severe to him, and he looked forward with satisfaction to his new duties.

On September 24., after various trifling postponements, he set off with a proper podoroschna (passport) from Krasnoi Pachri to travel post by Serpuchow, Tula, Riazan, Jaroslaw, and Novogrod to Petersburgh, there to fit himself out afresh, and proceed to Riga.

He was, however, arrested on the Oka, near Serpuchow, by the militia, for not speaking Russian. The podoroschna — a portmanteau full of Russian official correspondence — the Russian order for his new appointment — the uniform — all were insufficient to allay the suspicions of the militia: — a

German, or, as most thought, a Frenchman, with a Polish servant; this seemed to them too serious a matter. They forced the Author to return to headquarters with another officer on his way to the army. Not to fall again into this difficulty, the Author determined to wait for a courier, and accompany him. After some days it happened, that Count Chasot of the Prussian, and Baron Bode of the Saxon service, who had made the campaign in the suite of the hereditary Prince of Oldenburg, were to start for Petersburgh, with the commission to commence the raising of a German legion. They obtained a Russian feldjäger for their journey; and the Author resolved to accompany them. In some of the small towns we narrowly escaped on this journey, in despite of our feldjäger, the being again accused and detained as spies. Count Chasot was so ill on the road, that we were obliged generally to halt for the night; and our journey occupied a fortnight. We thus reached Petersburgh the middle of October.

As we presented ourselves in Jaroslaw to the second Prince of Oldenburg, who had returned to this his government, and was very active and useful in its administration, the Grand Duchess Catharine did us the honour to give us an audience.

The French had not yet commenced their retreat; but the conviction that they must and would commence it, had every where grown up and spread itself; and but few now thought of the possibility of a further offensive movement towards the south.

The Grand Duchess showed great curiosity for accounts from the army; she questioned us with much judgment and knowledge; and we saw how seriously she weighed all we could tell her. She asked the Author his opinion as to Buonaparte's expected movement; whether it would be a simple retreat? and on what road? The Author replied, that he did not doubt of the early retreat of the French army; and that he thought it would be made on the road by which they had advanced. The Grand Duchess appeared to have formed the same opinion. She conveyed to us the impression of a woman formed to govern.

As we now entirely quit the grand army, we may be allowed an observation on Buonaparte's retreat, in the point of view above mentioned.

We have never understood why it has been so obstinately contended, that Buonaparte should have taken another line for his retreat than the one by which he had advanced. From what could he draw his subsistence, but from his magazines? What could an " *unexhausted country* " do for an army which had no time to lose, and was forced to bivouac in great masses? what commissary could precede it to collect supplies? and what Russian authority would have obeyed his orders? The army would have been starved in a week.

A man who retires from an enemy's country requires, by all rules, a prepared route; one who retires under very difficult circumstances has double need of it; one who has to retire 120 miles in

Russia requires it threefold: by a prepared route, we mean one occupied by detachments, and in which magazines have been formed.

The march of Buonaparte on Kaluga was a very necessary beginning of his retreat, without the intermixture of the notion of another road. Kutusow, from Tarutino, had three marches less to Smolensko than Buonaparte from Moscow; the latter, therefore, was compelled to begin, by endeavouring to overwhelm the other, and gain the advance of him before he began his real retreat. It would, naturally, have been more advantageous to him, if he could have manœuvred Kutusow back to Kaluga. He hoped to effect this by suddenly passing from the old road to the new, whereby he menaced Kutusow's left flank. As this, however, and the attempt at Malo Jaroslawetz appeared failures, he made the best of it; and thought it no longer time, out of the few men who remained to him, to leave some 20,000 on the field of a general action, in order to end by retiring after all.

That in this manner Buonaparte began his retreat with an apparently new offensive movement directed towards the south, was a matter of much importance in his estimation, as we now know his character.

From the point where Buonaparte had to approach Kutusow, he had, indeed, to march a certain distance on a new road before he could reach the old. This, however, had not the same difficulties, since this fraction of his line lay sidewards, and between him

and his detachments on the Smolensko road. He
also prepared this route by sending Poniatowski
to the right, who also started by the reconquest of
Wereja. Buonaparte made this fraction as small
as possible. He did not retire from Malo Jaros-
lawety direct on Wiazma, because this route was
too much exposed; but retired on Borowsk, and
straight by Wereja to Mojaisk. Who can for an
instant doubt, that this movement was founded on
the most pressing motives?

When the Author arrived at Petersburgh, a change
had taken place in the government of Riga. The
Marquis Paulucci, of whom we have before spoken,
had relieved General Essen in that command. The
Author had the utmost reluctance to be attached to
this strange man. As, moreover, at this juncture,
the news arrived of the French retreat, and it was
to be anticipated that Riga would be out of the
circle of active hostilities, the Author applied to the
Duke of Oldenburg, who was in Petersburgh employed in raising the Russo-German legion, and
begged for the place of chief officer on his staff,
which had once before been thought of for him; in
the mean time, however, as, pending the formation
of the legion, this place would be an idle one, to
obtain for him the Emperor's leave to join General
Wittgenstein's army, and remain with it till the
legion should appear in the line of operations. The
Emperor granted this double request; and the
Author, after waiting a week for dispatches, left
Petersburgh on the 15th September, and travelled

by Pskow and Polozk to Czasnicki, the head-quarter of Wittgenstein, which he reached some days after the battle of Smoliany.

In Wittgenstein's head-quarters there reigned a kind of self-satisfaction—a proud consciousness of service performed — which somewhat contrasted with the head-quarters of the main army.

Petersburgh had been covered by Wittgenstein's operations, and this circumstance had obtained for him, besides the substantial rewards of the Emperor, a quantity of flattering eulogies from that capital, by which the halo of its glory was heightened in its lustre. In fact, there was reason to be satisfied with his campaign in all respects. He had always displayed himself morally equal, frequently superior to his adversary; he had thoroughly fulfilled the commission entrusted to him; and on this stage the result had remained adverse to France, and this not only by force of circumstances, but by the able dispositions of the Russian.

If we put together the three French corps which were consumed before Wittgenstein, Oudinot, St. Cyr, and Victor, and the cuirassier division of Doumerc at their original strength, we attain a total of 98,000 men. All who had fought under Wittgenstein did not certainly amount to 75,000. He had thus neutralised for the offensive a superior mass of the enemy, lost no ground, but on the contrary obtained such a superiority, that he was ready now to take part in the operation devised at Petersburgh for cutting off the French army. Such a result gained against French troops and Buona-parte's lieutenants deserves the name of a glorious campaign.

General Wittgenstein was a man some forty years of age, full of good will, activity, and enter-prise. His understanding was a little deficient in clearness, and his activity in solid energy.

The chief of his staff was the Major-general d'Auvray, a Saxon by birth, who had long served in Russia, and was upwards of fifty. He was a well-humoured man of the noblest character, and had an active and cultivated mind. Honourable and full of zeal, he was always impelled by public con-siderations. He was a little deficient in practical sol-diership. He was not to be trifled with, and could lay about him on occasion, which is often necessary.

Major-general Diebitsch was Quarter-master-general. A Prussian by birth, he had early left the school of cadets there for the Russian service, and had risen to the rank of colonel rapidly through the guards and the staff, so that in the course of this campaign he became a general in his twenty-seventh year. He was the prime mover in the army of Wittgenstein.

He had been diligent in his youth and had ac-quired much knowledge in his profession. Fiery, brave, and enterprising; quick in resolve; of great firmness, with good natural understanding; some-what confident and imperious; carrying others along with him, and very ambitious; such was General Diebitsch; and these qualities carried him on rapidly to his ends. As he had a noble heart, was honest and open, without a trace of intrigue, both Wittgenstein and D'Auvray soon acknowledged his sway. We see that Wittgenstein's head-quarter was composed of three very important men, full of honest zeal and good will, without sinister views; that there was no want of acuteness or fire; and we shall find that the incidents of Wittgenstein's campaign correspond to such a composition, if candidly and practically considered.

The Author reached the army at the moment when it had just repulsed the last attempt of the French marshals to attack it near Smoliany. It looked on this affair as a newly won victory, and in this tone we heard of seventeen pitched battles spoken of as having been fought by Wittgenstein's army. This was only a mode of expressing the great activity which had reigned on this theatre of the war. The victory of Smoliany was, however, considered as a mere defensive action, which did not admit of being prosecuted so as to become an important passage of the campaign.

In pursuance of instructions from the Emperor, Wittgenstein had to press Oudinot altogether away from this district, to throw him back on Wilna, and then to leave it to the army of Steinheil to keep him out of play. Without stopping to remark on the strange confusion of these instructions, we will only observe that this did not happen. Oudinot had retired on Victor to the country between the Dnieper and Dwina; the 6th corps alone, still consisting of 2000 men, had diverged towards Wilna; and Steinheil was not in condition to form a separate army, but could do nothing better than join himself to Wittgenstein.

Wittgenstein was only 40,000 strong; Oudinot and Victor were estimated at least at that number. Some troops were also required to oppose Wrede; and Wittgenstein was consequently in this manner sufficiently occupied if he hindered the French from doing more than stand against him.

Beyond this the instructions were that Wittgenstein was to occupy the Ula from Lepel downwards, and then wait for further events. Wittgenstein, according to this, had no occasion to leave the neighbourhood of Czasnicki. He remained quiet, therefore, for a week after the action of Smoliany. On November 20th he learned that the marshals opposed to him were making a movement towards the Beresina, which indicated the approach of the French main army, respecting which nothing more was here known than that it had arrived in a very weakened state at Smolensko. Wittgenstein resolved to let his advanced guard, now on the roads of Czereja and Kolopodniczi, pursue the enemy closely, and to march with his main body on Czereja, where he remained in a direction calculated to cover the Ula, and to lie in wait for Buonaparte behind that river should he take this direction.

On the 22d he heard of Tchitschagow's arrival at Borissow. He was required by this general to draw near enough to that point for them to act together. General Wittgenstein marched hereupon towards Kolopodniczi. Here he heard of the battle of Krasnoi, that Buonaparte had been in Orza on the 19th, and that Kutusow had halted for some days, and sent only an advanced guard of 20,000 men in pursuit, which followed the French army at the distance of one day's march. An account came in at the same time of a very disadvantageous affair which the division of Tchitschagow's army under Pahlen had sustained on the 23d on the left bank of the Beresina.

The threads were now gathering up into the final knot. The Beresina at Borissow, and for a day's march above and below that point, was closed by the Admiral's army. From local knowledge it might be assumed with tolerable certainty that the French army had no means of forcing a passage within these limits. It was therefore believed that it would be forced to turn to the right or the left, and take its way either by Lepel or Bobruisk. Under these circumstances it seemed probable that it would prefer Bobruisk, since towards Lepel Wittgenstein was in its way. Wittgenstein, however, who was by his instructions supposed responsible both for Lepel and the Ula, was obliged to keep the latter in view, and thus to maintain such a position that he could await the enemy either on the road to Lepel or behind the Ula; he could not, therefore, cross the Beresina in order to unite himself with Tchitschagow.

The surest way of securing a share in the transaction, would certainly have been for him to have advanced on the 25th and 26th direct on the great road from Smolensko to Borissow. Had Buonaparte turned to the left, he would have been nearer to him; had he remained on this road, or marched towards Lepel, Wittgenstein might have attacked him, and deranged his plans.

Wittgenstein, however, had lately had two French marshals opposed to him, whose united strength he reckoned nearly equal to his own; if one of these had turned towards Borissow, he would still have been on the left bank of the river, and easily supported by the other. The main French army, advancing under Buonaparte's personal command, was according to some accounts still 80,000 strong, and at the lowest computation then current 60,000. We must not wonder at this over-estimate. It was known, indeed, that the French had suffered enormous losses, but still 60,000 were not reckoned much by those who remembered that, three months before, 300,000 men had advanced on this very road. The last official accounts received of the enemy's strength, dated from before the actions near Krasnoi. It had then been much overrated by Kutusow, and it was impossible to estimate with accuracy its losses in these actions. Observation by reconnaissance was very difficult, for it was impossible to distinguish in the moving mass those still bearing arms from others. In short it is both conceivable and excusable, that in Wittgenstein's head-quarters it should have been supposed, that a mass of from 90,000 to 100,000 men was in their front; whereas we now know that it consisted of about 30,000.

From the Admiral, Wittgenstein could expect no succour; he was chained to an extended defensive position; he had besides received so smart a slap in the face on his attempt to cross, that it was to be foreseen he would not expose himself to a second. The Russian main army had given up immediate pursuit; even its advanced guard was two marches behind. Wittgenstein therefore was much left to himself, and could reckon on no support for the first day of an action, and was very uncertain of any for the second. Under such circumstances to go blindly forward was the leap of Curtius into the gulph.

Had Wittgenstein on the 25th made a march direct from Kolopodniczi on Borissow, and on the 26th attacked every thing he found before him, he would not have found the gulf so deep as he apprehended. He might have been beaten by Buonaparte, but he would have hindered his passage for a day, and perhaps for two. But this self-sacrifice for the general good, which sounds so well in books, is nevertheless not to be reckoned on in the practice of the world, or only at least in a few cases, where, on sufficient authority, it takes the shape of an indispensable duty.

From General Diebitsch we had expected a bold and self-forgetting rush forward: how far he advocated such, and failed, we could not learn; but it was easy to observe that unity did not prevail at head-quarters at this crisis.

Wittgenstein acted as most men in his place would have acted; and not in a manner to be absolutely condemned. He marched on the 25th from Kolopedniczi on the road from Borissow to Lepel, and kept the first place occupied, by which he commanded the way to the upper Beresina and the Ula. As his advanced guards did not touch on the enemy on the 25th, he saw plainly that Buonaparte had not turned to the right, and he therefore, on the 26th, made a march towards the Borrissow road to Kostritza, a place which is only two leagues from that road, and two miles from the point where the French contemplated their passage.

At Kostritza, Wittgenstein learned that the French were taking measures to effect their passage at Studianka. As Tschitschagow had occupied the country as far as Zembin, the result of this attempt to force a passage appeared very doubtful. Wittgenstein, however, determined on the 27th to move forward on the road, and attack the enemy in their rear, while occupied by Tschitschagow in front.

The Author was not at this moment at head-quarters, but with a detachment left behind to cover the left flank, and only reached the army on the evening of the 28th. He had not therefore occasion to observe in person the course of the conflicts with Victor on the 27th and 28th; and the reason was not made clear to him, from actual observation, why Wittgenstein marched not on Studianka, but on the Smolensko road, while he knew that the former was the point selected by the enemy to cross. Unquestionably this exhibited a certain timidity, a too great anxiety to preserve his corps from all injury; and on this occasion, General Wittgenstein cannot be acquitted of a certain share in the escape of Buonaparte. On the 27th he could not indeed have absolutely hindered the passage, but he might have made the French loss much greater.

Wittgenstein made some 10,000 prisoners on these two days, and among them an entire division. With this brilliant result he soothed his conscience, and transferred the blame to Tschitschagow, who had abandoned the ground as far as Zembin at an unlucky moment.

The latter general seems certainly to have exhibited no great capacity for command in this campaign. It is however true, that every man was possessed with the idea, that the enemy would take the direction of Bobruisk. Even from Kutusow advices were forwarded to this effect. The notion that the neighbourhood of Wittgenstein would hinder him from turning to the right was the main origin of this preconceived opinion. The admiral had, however, full time, after his false movement on the 27th, to have disputed the passage, and in this lies the main charge against him.

Never were circumstances more propitious towards reducing an army to capitulate in the field. The Beresina fenced in, partly by morass, and partly by dense forest, affords means of passage, *and of afterwards continuing a march* only at a few points. The enemy was only 30,000 strong, about as many Russians were behind the river, as many more in front, and 10,000 more on the march to join them from behind. In addition to this utter dissolution of order in the enemy's ranks, 40,000 disarmed stragglers, hunger, sickness, and exhaustion of moral and physical force.

Chance certainly somewhat favoured Buonaparte in his discovery near Borissow of a place so favourable for the passage as Studianka; but it was his reputation which chiefly saved him, and he traded in this instance on a capital amassed long before. Wittgenstein and Tschitschagow were both afraid of him here, as Kutusow had been afraid of him at Krasnoi, of him, of his army, of his guard. No one chose to be defeated by him. Kutusow believed he could obtain his end without that risk: Wittgenstein was reluctant to impair the glory he had acquired, Tschitschagow to undergo a second check.

Buonaparte was endowed with this moral strength when he thus extricated himself from one of the worst situations in which a general ever found himself. This moral power, however, was not all; the strength of his intellect, and the military virtues of his army, which not even its calamities could quite subdue, were destined here to show themselves once more in their full lustre. After he had overcome all the difficulties of this perilous moment,

Buonaparte said to those about him, " Vous voyez comme on passe sous la barbe de l'ennemi."

Buonaparte had here entirely saved his old honour and acquired new, but the result was still a stride towards the utter destruction of his army. We know how much of it reached Kowno, and that the Beresina contributed the last blow towards this result. Besides himself, his principal generals, and a couple of thousand officers, he brought away nothing of the whole army worth mentioning. When, therefore, we speak of his bringing the difficult retreat to a stand, the expression is but a name, and this is the case with the individual incidents of the retreat. Eugene escaped by a detour at Krasnoi, but with half his troops. Ney escaped likewise by a greater circuit, with 600 men out of 6000 (as his secretary relates). Nominally, the Russians had failed in cutting off their enemy; Eugene, Ney, at Krasnoi, Buonaparte at the Beresina; but, nevertheless, they had cut off considerable masses. This holds still more true of the campaign as a whole. The Russians seldom head the French; when they do so they let them through. The French are every where victorious; but look to the end of the account, the French army has ceased to exist, and, with the exception of the capture of Buonaparte and his principal lieutenants, the campaign has the most complete result conceivable. Should the Russian army be denied all merit for this? That were gross injustice.

Never was a pursuit conducted with such activity and exertion. The Russian generals were certainly often timid at moments when they should have clutched the fugitives, but still the energy of the pursuit was wonderful. We must consider the scale of operations. In November and December, in the ice and snow of Russia, after an arduous campaign, either by side roads little beaten, or on the main road utterly devastated, under great difficulties of subsistence, the following an enemy 120 miles in 50 days is perhaps without example; and, to exemplify in a word the entire magnitude of the exertion, we have only to say that the Russian army marched out of Tarutino 110,000 strong, and entered Wilna 40,000. The rest had remained behind, dead, wounded, or exhausted. This exertion did great honour to Kutusow.

When at Krasnoi, he at last resolved to descend upon his adversary, when he showed an intention of blocking his road to the Dnieper, with the half of his own army under Tormasow, and then, in the moment of execution of the long expected blow, held in his strength, and suffered the dreaded fugitive to escape with a moderate squeeze, then men believed they witnessed either the extreme of weakness, or a dangerous indifference for the honour and success of the Russian arms. Such men, however, in truth, reasoned rather in their chamber than on the field of battle of Krasnoi.

Let such reflect on the winter in all its inhospitality, on shattered powers, physical and moral, an army led from bivouac to bivouac, suffering from privation, decimated by sickness, its path strewn with dead, dying, and exhausted bodies,—they will comprehend with what difficulty each motion was accomplished, and how nothing but the strongest impulses could overcome the inertia of the mass.

Kutusow saw his army melting in his grasp, and the difficulty he would have in bringing any considerable portion of it to the frontier. He saw that the result of the campaign must in any case be a colossal one; he foresaw with much acuteness the total destruction of his enemy: " Tout cela se fondra sans moi," were his words to those about him. Could an accelerated catastrophe, or rather, ought it, have such a value in his eyes as to make him put a portion of his own remaining strength to hazard. That the personal apprehension of being once more soundly beaten by Buonaparte was one of his strongest motives, we do not intend to question; but if we dismiss the motive, does not enough remain to make his caution intelligible? Neither should we overlook the fact that he estimated the strength of his enemy higher than it was.

Kutusow determined not to throw his whole strength upon his adversary, but to follow him unceasingly with great and small detachments, to harass and exhaust him. This he deemed sufficient for his object. Most commanders in his place would so have reasoned.

In one point only can we charge him with absolute error. He knew that Tschitschagow and

Wittgenstein had waylaid Buonaparte on the Beresina, and would bring him to a stand. This was in the plan laid down by the Emperor. Under these circumstances it was his business for the moment to keep within a march of the French army. If then the halt of two days at Krasnoi were indispensable, he should have made up for lost time by two forced marches, in order to come up with the enemy at Borissow, which the latter reached on the 25th and 26th, on the 27th, instead of which he was at Krugloe four marches distant. His advanced guard reached Borissow on the 28th. He took himself a direction straight for Minsk by Usoza. As it was a question here not of more or less ultimate success, but of support to his subordinates, his conduct is liable to a different judgment from that which concerns the affair of Krasnoi.

From the Beresina, Tschitschagow took the lead in the pursuit, followed by Miloradowitsch. Platoff and several other Cossack corps hung on the French flanks, or even gained their front. As Wittgenstein in this state of things was useless on the great road, which also was in a fearful state, he quitted it at Kamen, and took his direction to Niemenzin, situated on the bend which the Wilia makes to the north above Wilna. We, therefore, saw only a fraction of the famous line of retreat, but on this fraction of some three days' march, all the horrors of that movement were accumulated. So many descriptions of the miseries of the French army have been published, that the author deems an additional stroke of the pencil superfluous. It is true, that he felt as if he could never be released from the horrible impressions of the spectacle. He will mention but one circumstance. Let no one overlook the hardships with which the Russian soldier had, as well as the French, to contend. In the middle of an unusually severe winter, the corps were generally compelled to bivouac; for the few wretched villages within reach of the road, such as exist in this part of Lithuania, could receive but few troops, and were generally appropriated of necessity to the cavalry. If all were then to be in quarters, the force must have been divided into far smaller columns. Subsistence was also very scanty, since we could not send on far in advance, and our continual progress made it impossible to bring in supplies from any distance on the flanks. We saw then the road which had been passed even by the advanced guard continually marked out by the bodies of Russians, who had sunk under the cold and the fatigue. Wittgenstein lost in the last four weeks a good fourth of his force, for he had left Czasnicki 40,000 strong, and reached Wilna with scarce 30,000.

Wittgenstein received from head-quarters an order to move on Samogitia and the lower Niemen, in order to cut off Macdonald, who as it appeared had not yet withdrawn from Courland.

In fact, Buonaparte had not thought of forwarding the order for this general's retreat, and it was first despatched from Wilna to him, through the

King of Naples, being committed to a Prussian officer who was then in Wilna. This man, not in himself very trustworthy, and induced by his apprehensions to make a great circuit by Tilsit and Teltsch, reached Mittau only on the 18th December.

Macdonald had been in a state of painful disquietude. Another Prussian officer had been sent by General York to General Krusemark at Wilna, had left it again on the 6th, as the first fugitives arrived from the grand army, and had reached General York on the 10th, with the news of the Emperor's retreat, and the dissolution of the French army. Marshal Macdonald and General York were already on very bad terms, and the former thought it beneath his dignity to make particular inquiries into these accounts. He expected every hour to receive official reports from Wilna, and declared, in the mean time, that the reports current were inventions of ill will to the cause. Macdonald was, meanwhile, the more uneasy, because two thirds of his corps were Prussians, and he no longer placed any confidence in General York.

On the 18th December the officer arrived from Wilna with the order to march, but also with the confirmation of the worst reports. On the 19th, Macdonald moved in four columns. Two consisted of the division Grandjean and six battalions, ten squadrons and two batteries, Prussian, under General Massenbach ; the other two, of the remainder of the Prussians under Generals York and Kleist.

The two first, with the Marshal at their head, marched a day earlier than the others, and preserved this interval. The road was common to both by Janischki, Schawlia, and Koltiniani; from the latter the one column marched by Tauroggen and Piktupöhnen, the other by Pojour, Coadjuten, and Rucken, towards Tilsit. The Marshal remained with the latter.

The march was tolerably rapid; for the two first columns, which moved on the 19th December, reached Piktupöhnen and its neighbourhood in eight days, which is thirty miles from Mittau. Much snow, frost, and bad roads, increased the difficulties of this march. Under these circumstances, General York, who had left Mittau only on the evening of the 20th, and brought with him a long train of baggage, and the two remaining columns, came up to within two marches of Macdonald. He reached, namely, on the evening of the 25th, the neighbourhood of Koltiniani. On this day, however, the Marshal was at Wainuti, six miles distant.

This remaining behind of General York can scarcely be considered as adopted with ulterior designs, but rather as sufficiently accounted for by circumstances of the moment.

Wittgenstein, after having given his corps some days' rest at Niemenzin, had moved thence on the 17th December, and taken the direction of Georgenburg on the Niemen, by Wilkomir and Keidany.

He had, besides his usual advanced guard, two smaller corps, principally of cavalry, under General Scheppelow, further in advance. The one under Major-General Kutusow consisted of 4000 men, infantry and cavalry, and was on the 20th, while Wittgenstein was at Wilkomir, already six marches further, at Georgenburg, the crossing place of the river. The other, of which the quarter-master-general, General Diebitsch, had meanwhile taken the command, in whose suite the author now found himself, consisted of the regiment of Grodno Hussars, three regiments of Cossacks, together 1300 horse, a Jäger regiment, which mustered, however, only 120 men and 6 guns, light artillery.

This corps was already at Koltiniani on the 20th, seven marches, therefore, from Wittgenstein, and in the direction of Memel. General Diebitsch had yet obtained no accounts of Macdonald's situation, and did not doubt that he had taken the direction of Memel, with a view of crossing the Curische Haf.* In this case Diebitsch could have done

---

* A few years ago travellers from Petersburgh to Berlin usually preferred, to the Tilsit road, that which leads from Memel to Konigsberg by the Curische Haf, and which now the improvement of the southern route has, we believe, thrown entirely into disuse. Those who have performed this fraction of the wearying journey above mentioned will not easily forget the desert aspect of this narrow strip of land, and the risk which carriages usually incurred of being upset into the Baltic by the occasional quicksand, which the postilion preferred encountering to the fatigue of wading through the more uniformly loose accumulation of drift at a higher level. Under the hot sun of the short summer of northern Europe, it required the motion of a

nothing with him. His present view was to cross Samogitia, and summon the town of Memel. After passing Teltsch, and when distant only two marches from Memel, he suddenly learned, on the 23d, that Macdonald had by no means executed his retreat, but was now on the march on the Schawlia road. The account seemed to him scarcely credible; other accounts, however, arrived to confirm it, and Diebitsch turned back at once, and marched upon Worni. Here, on the 25th, he heard that Macdonald's rear-guard was in Wengkowa, and he determined to waylay him the next day at Koltiniani. He marched early, and reached this point at 10 A. M. We fell in with some Prussian sutlers belonging to Massenbach's corps: they told us that a rear-guard of two squadrons of Hussars and two companies of Jägers were still behind, but that all the rest had marched through. General Diebitsch made his dispositions to cut off this rear-guard.

The Author, who had two brothers with the Prussian corps, of whom the one was a major and commanded the Jägers attached to it, could guess, with much probability, that as a good outpost officer he would have the command of this rear-guard. The thought of seeing him here taken prisoner was more painful than that of being opposed to him under fire through the day. It was then an indescribable satisfaction to him to

carriage to convince the traveller that he was not creeping along the coast of Syria. A camel for this day's journey would have been a more appropriate means of transport.

learn from stragglers brought in that the rear-guard consisted of four battalions of infantry, two squadrons of cavalry and a battery, and was commanded by General Kleist.

General Diebitsch at the head of 1400 men, far from any support, had certainly no intention of meddling seriously with such a body; he wished, however, like a player at ombre, to play a small trump, in order to see how the cards lay. He asked the Author, whether he would ride with a flag of truce to General Kleist. The Author replied, that as a Russian officer, he was ready to undertake any duty assigned to him; but that it would be more agreeable to him, if General Diebitsch would send on this service a Livonian or a Courlander, who could speak German as well, and who would probably be less unacceptable, on a first impression, to General Kleist, than one of the Prussian officers who had left the Prussian service at the first outbreak of hostilities, to the great annoyance of most of the Prussian chiefs. General Diebitsch admitted these reasons, and sent the Major v. Reune on this mission.

This officer was to represent to General Kleist, that his direct road was occupied by a considerable detachment; that means might be found to come to an understanding, and avoid useless bloodshed; and that General Diebitsch, therefore, wished to have a conference with General Kleist.

The Major v. Reune returned with the answer, that General Kleist could admit of no conference, since he was not the commander ; that General York himself was still behind, and would arrive in the evening; that, till then, the transaction might remain as it was. It was now evident that we had separated, not a rear-guard, but the whole Prussian corps, from Macdonald.

General Diebitsch might think himself fortunate to have been led hither by events. In a military view, he could promise himself no advantages, or at best trifling ones, from his position; but the possibility of coming to an understanding with the Prussians was of the highest value.

The position of the various corps on this day was as follows: —

General York, and Kleist, with 10,000 men, half a mile east of Koltiniani.

In their front, General Diebitsch, with 1400 men, at Koltiniani.

Macdonald, with some 4000 men, at Wainuti, six miles from Koltiniani, on the western road towards Tilsit.

Grandjean, with 6000 men, at Tauroggen, four miles from Koltiniani, and about as far from Wainuti, on the eastern road to Tilsit.

General Kutusow, with 4000 men, at Piktupöhnen, on the road from Tauroggen to Tilsit; he had also occupied Tilsit.

General Scheppelow, the real advanced guard of Wittgenstein, 4000 strong, at Wielona; still one march distant from Georgenburg.

Finally, Count Wittgenstein, with some 15,000 men; one march further back towards Keidany.

On the following day, the 26th, when General York should have continued his march by Koltiniani, the above distribution was changed, in so far as each corps made a march forward towards its object. General Kutusow alone stood fast; and his position at Piktupöhnen, where General Wlastow commanded, was, in consequence, attacked by the Prussian cavalry, forming part of the advanced guard of General Grandjean, and driven back, with the loss of two weak battalions and some artillery, upon Tilsit, where General Kutusow rallied the beaten troops.

Kutusow now moved to Ragnit, on the left bank of the Niemen, two miles above Tilsit; and Piktupöhnen, which is a kind of a defile, as well as Tilsit, were both occupied by the French.

Macdonald was with his force at Coadjuten, one march north-west of Piktupöhnen.

We see that General York was certainly destitute of all near support; still a detachment of 1300 horse was not in condition seriously to dispute his passage. He had, indeed, two heavy marches to make, before he could reach Grandjean at Piktupöhnen, or Macdonald at Coadjuten; and the Russian cavalry would have captured a good many of his waggons, and caused him other losses, as he was too weak in cavalry to keep General Diebitsch entirely at a distance ; finally, he could not be assured that other Russian detachments, or even

Wittgenstein himself, might not arrive. These considerations, however, under different circumstances, would not have caused General York to pause for an instant.

Macdonald began, on the 25th, to be very uneasy as to his position. On the one hand, reports were current, that Tilsit and Piktupöhnen were already in the hands of the Russians; on the other, he had no advices from General York. In order not to abandon him entirely, he made, on the 26th, a small march towards Coadjuten of two miles; and on the 27th another of the like distance, in the direction of Tilsit to Schillgallen. He reached Tilsit only on the 28th, and remained there the 29th, although he had reason for great anxiety as to his further retreat. In these four days he believed that, without doubt, he must fall in with General York, and waited anxiously for news of him. Several attempts to communicate with him failed, though made with strong patroles, being prevented by the Russian cavalry.

We turn now to General York: he joined General Kleist towards evening with the remainder of the corps, and sent word to General Diebitsch, by the officer who had been again sent to him, that he was ready to hold a conference between the outposts. This took place at nightfall.

We must here dwell for an instant on General York and his position.

General York was a man some fifty years of age, distinguished for bravery and military talent. He had served in his youth in the Dutch colonies, had seen the world, and enlarged the sphere of his intellectual observation. A fiery and passionate will, concealed beneath apparent coldness; a powerful ambition, suppressed by constant resignation; and strength and boldness of character distinguished him. He was honest; but gloomy, choleric, and reserved, and a bad subordinate. Personal attachment was not congenial to him. The stimulus of his actions was fame, and the means were supplied by strong natural abilities. His worst feature was, that under the appearance of being downright and straightforward he was, in fact, close and reserved. He talked loud when his hopes were lowest, and assumed despondency when he entertained no apprehension.

He was unquestionably one of the most distinguished men of our army. Scharnhorst, who recognised his availability at a moment when few had shown themselves available, and valued it the more because it was connected with a great aversion for the French, had always endeavoured to keep on good terms with him, although York always entertained against him a suppressed venom. From time to time this seemed ready to break out; but Scharnhorst made as if he did not perceive it, and pushed him forward wherever a man of his kind could be made useful.

On the breaking out of the Russian war, the French requested the appointment of General Grawert, who was old and infirm, of limited ability and energy, and, moreover, of old, not disinclined to French interests in Europe. The King thought himself obliged to defer to Buonaparte's desire. Scharnhorst, who had ostensibly retired, but still played a card in the game, brought to bear the appointment of General York as second in command. He represented to the King, that Grawert, a man old in years and feeble in character, would easily be led to give way too far to the French, that a man of character and determination was required for the post, and that no one was more fit for it than York. He was, therefore, attached to the corps of Grawert, with the rank of lieutenant-general, and was, in fact, a supervisor of Grawert's proceedings.

The latter, at the end of six weeks, became so sick in body and feeble in mind, that he was obliged to give up the command to York. In a very short time, York and Macdonald became on bad terms. Macdonald's Courland campaign was certainly not of a nature to command approbation. While with the 7th division he occupied an idle position on the Dwina, the Prussians remained in a very indifferent one before Riga, and had to sustain, unsupported for the most part, the actions which occurred during six months of the campaign. General York was not an indulgent observer; for bitterness was a predominant feature in his composition. The consequence was, that he was dissatisfied with the measures of the Marshal, quite as much with reference to affairs in general as with regard to the Prussian corps; and on the other hand, perhaps, had too strong a feeling of pride at the performances of the Prussian contingent. His cold, reserved, and mistrustful demeanour, and the expressions of those about him, left the Marshal not long in doubt; and the cloud soon rose thick between them. The subsistence of the troops, which at first had been managed by a Prussian commissary, and afterwards under a French one had sensibly deteriorated, brought the ill humours to words. York complained of want of forage; and Macdonald asserted, that his horses were bursting with over feeding. The affair came, in the course of a short correspondence, to bitter language; and the Marshal formally accused York of want of zeal and good will for the cause. Both made their reports of the transaction, which occurred towards the end of November, to Wilna—York to the Prussian minister, General Krusemark, the Marshal to the Duke of Bassano. York sent also to Berlin one of his aide-de-camps to give the King intelligence of the circumstances. This officer had not returned when York was to hold his first conference with General Diebitsch.

Although General York, on receiving his appointment, had been furnished with a special instruction, it is nevertheless certain, that this instruction contained nothing by which the step he had now in contemplation could be justified.

General Essen, so long ago as in September, had, with a view of proving General York, earnestly pressed for an interview at the outposts, which was granted. The demeanour, however, of the Prussian general was probably too imposing; for General Essen had not courage enough to explain himself, and nothing came under discussion. The Marquis Paulucci was a man of bolder speech; and the circumstances of the beginning of December were more propitious to freedom of language. On the 5th of December he formally summoned General York to defection. The latter, indeed, rejected the demand; but offered himself as the intermediary, if the Emperor had any propositions to make to the King through the Marquis. Proposals followed through this medium, but couched in general language. General York forwarded them to Berlin through his aide-de-camp, the Major von Seydlitz.

It is necessary to advert to all these circumstances in order to place in full light the step of General York.

He was too prudent a man to let himself be guided in this transaction by his mere animosity against Marshal Macdonald: this would have been the application of enormous means to a little end, and would have led him far beyond his object. On the other hand, however, it is conceivable, that a friendly relation between the two generals, a man in York's place, of the good-natured qualities which belonged to the Marshal, and a real devotion of the subordinate towards the person of the chief, might perhaps have operated to prevent the remarkable occurrence which took place.

The feelings of the King and his people towards

the French could be no secret to General York. Whether, however, the catastrophe which the French had incurred would be considered at Berlin as a perfect change of the balance, and the moment as one favourable for a sudden conversion of the part played by Prussia in the drama, these were questions General York was unable to resolve.

If he stopped to reflect on the state of things at Berlin, he had to anticipate the most decided aversion to such sudden change. Scharnhorst, the most determined enemy of the French, and the man who would have given such counsel and supported it to the last, was removed from the ministry, and living in Silesia. Baron Hardenberg had shown dexterity in steering between breakers, but it was much to be doubted whether he could either adopt for himself an hearty and high resolution, or instil one into others. For General York, therefore, now to adopt for himself, and at his own risk, a resolution, which must drag with it the policy of Prussia in a directly opposite direction to the one now prevailing, would be to embrace one of the boldest lines of conduct recorded in history. Count Haugwitz had, it is true, permitted himself something of the same kind in 1805, when he concluded the Vienna treaty, but Count Haugwitz then acted in the interest of the more powerful party at home, and knew that Prussia opposed itself to that party with reluctance; neither is a diplomatic act of boldness ever so severely resented as a military one. In the one case it costs a place, in the other a head, according to rules. If the King were determined to adhere to his alliance with France, no course remained for him but to bring General York to trial.

The reader will forgive a dissertation, so long and so often interrupted, on an event so small in comparison with the magnitude of his whole subject as the transaction between Generals York and Diebitsch up to this moment. It is only now that we believe we have arrived at a point from which we can contemplate the occurrence in the real extent of its relations, and we return to Koltiniani.

The conference took place, as we have mentioned, on the evening of the 25th. General Diebitsch had placed his troops so as to conceal his force as much as possible, but he was frank enough honourably to communicate the exact extent of the force at his disposal. He added, that he could not hope with such means absolutely to close the road of General York's retreat, but that he would do his best to cut off his train, his artillery waggons, and, possibly, some of his artillery. This argument was naturally the lightest which General Diebitsch had to adduce to give weight to his representations. The main subject of the discussion was the total destruction of the French army; and the circumstance that the Russian generals had received instructions from the Emperor to avoid, under probable circumstances, treating the Prussians as decided enemies, but, with reference to former friendly relations, and the likelihood of their early

renewal, to adopt every means for promoting such
an accommodation as might be agreeable to them.
General Diebitsch, in accordance with this, declared
his readiness to enter into an agreement for the
neutrality of the Prussians, and for this object to
give up any military advantages of his present
position.

General York made no decisive declaration in
reply. He showed an inclination towards an
agreement of such a nature as might leave the
honour of his arms untouched, but he was of
opinion that at this moment as a soldier he could
hardly be justified in accepting any. It was hereupon settled that no further military attempt should
be made on either side during the night; that in
the morning General York should make a *reconnoissance* and a march on Lawkowo, as with the
intention of turning the left of General Diebitsch,
but that the latter was to appear again in his front
at Schelel.

General York said to General Diebitsch at the
close of the conference, "You have a number of
Prussian officers with you — send me one of them
in future, and I shall have more confidence."

General Diebitsch, on this invitation, asked the
Author whether he would undertake the office, as
suggested, to which the Author could only reply
in the affirmative.

It was late when we returned to Koltiniani,
perhaps towards ten o'clock. General Diebitsch
spoke with the Author upon what had happened,

and asked him what he thought of General York's views, and what kind of man he was. The Author could not avoid warning General Diebitsch of General York's close disposition. He was much afraid that the General might make use of the night to put us to the rout, and pursue his way to Macdonald; he recommended, therefore, the utmost vigilance.

General Diebitsch placed two of his regiments of Cossacks in front of General York; the third to the rear, towards Schelel; and kept the hussar regiment in that place itself, which is tolerably spacious. The cavalry horses were kept bridled, and the orderlies at head-quarters were directed to observe the same precaution with theirs. We had dismounted at a house, had laid ourselves down on straw without undressing, and had just closed our eyes, when pistol shots were fired in the village and in our rear. They were not single shots, but a general discharge, which lasted some minutes. We sprung up, and the Author said to himself, "There is York on our rear—I guessed him rightly." We mounted. A couple of regiments were led to where the road issued from the town; they found, however, no enemy, but only the Cossack regiment which had to cover our rear. From these we learned that a troop of enemy's cavalry had ridden in amongst them, and thrown themselves into the village. It was, in fact, a patrole of fifty Prussian dragoons, which General Massenbach had sent under Captain Weiss from Schelel to Koltiniani, to

bring over a dispatch from Marshal Macdonald to
General York. Its orders were to cut its way to
the latter; but finding the opposition too strong,
after driving the Cossacks back into Koltiniani, it
had gone about, and disappeared, without leaving
a trace of its course. These circumstances we
learned afterwards from Prussian officers—for the
moment we were left in complete uncertainty.

General York made his *reconnoissance* on the
26th, but found it not advisable to make his flanking march in the direction previously settled, but
inclined on the way towards Schelel, which is the
road to Tilsit. The reason was the badness of the
roads, and the wish to avoid unnecessary annoyance
to his people and horses. General Diebitsch, however, was unavoidably suspicious, and believed that
the object was to gain a march towards Tilsit. A
lively interchange of flags of truce was the result,
in which the Author was constantly employed.

On the first occasion on which he was sent to
General York, that officer would not see him, for
fear of compromising himself. He reprimanded
the officer at the outposts for having allowed the
Author to penetrate so far without his special permission. The Author then did not see the General.
This, however, was a comedy: General York sent
to him the Russian Lieutenant-Colonel, Count
Dohna, to discuss the circumstances with him.

Count Dohna, like the Author, had left the
Prussian service for the Russian in 1812: he
belonged to the Russo-German legion, and had

received permission to go to Riga, in order to take part in the campaign. He was attached to General Lewis, who had followed General York's march with 5000 men from the Riga garrison, but was still several marches in the rear, and had sent forward Count Dohna as a negotiator. The Author was much rejoiced to recognise here one of his most intimate friends.

From what Count Dohna said, it appeared that General York meant honourably, but that he had an interest in postponing the transaction for a couple of days, and meanwhile could not remain nailed to one spot; that it was therefore necessary to admit of a movement further towards the Prussian frontier.

It was easy to understand this interest of the General; for besides that he was expecting the return of an aide-de-camp from Berlin, who arrived on the 29th, it would bear a better military appearance that he should make one or more attempts to unite himself with Macdonald. Had the latter remained in Tauroggen and Wainuti, where he was on the 25th, or returned thither on the 26th, nothing would have come of the convention. As Macdonald, however, continued his march, and as the Russians had remained between them, and could therefore prevent all communication between the French and Prussians, York could assume the appearance of having been deserted by Macdonald.

General Diebitsch saw this clearly enough; on the other hand, however, he was not sure of

General York; and should the latter manœuvre
him back on Tilsit, and master that place by a *coup
de main*, General Diebitsch would have played but
a poor part, and be placed in a questionable light.

General Diebitsch endeavoured, therefore, as
much as possible, to bring General York to a
decision, and protested without ceasing against a
further retreat. General York, however, endeavoured to appease him, and advanced upon him
continually, although by very short marches. In
this manner Diebitsch retired to Schelel the 26th,
Pagermont the 27th, and by Tauroggen to Willkischken the 28th, only two miles from Tilsit.
Macdonald with his last detachment had entered
Tilsit on this day, where he intended to wait for
York, who had reached Tauroggen. Nothing, in
fact, impeded now their junction but a light
cordon of Cossacks.

The transaction would now have been despaired
of, had not General York been already seriously
compromised by his slow progress and frequent
parleys. In a personal point of view, he could
hardly now back out of the business.

On the 29th the Author was sent once more to
General York at Tauroggen, whom he had left
only the night before in that place. On this
occasion he brought two written communications,
which were to be considered as an ultimatum.

The first was addressed to General Diebitsch by
General D'Auvray, chief of the staff to the Wittgenstein army, and contained some reproaches for

not having sooner brought the transaction with General York to a conclusion. The dispositions of the army were then communicated to him, by which it appeared that Wittgenstein's proper advanced guard under General Scheppelow was to be at Schillupischken on the 31st, Wittgenstein himself at Sommeran.

Schillupischken lies on the western road, from Tilsit to Königsberg. This road passes through the forest, in which, for the space of four miles, it forms frequent defiles. At Schillupischken itself, where it crosses a rivulet, there is a narrow pass; and Sommeran, where Wittgenstein intended to be, is only one mile from Schillupischken. Should Wittgenstein really accomplish his march, as he intended, and should Macdonald determine to wait for York in Tilsit, which place York could not reach before late in the evening of the 30th, it became doubtful whether both together would ever reach the forest. It is true that Wittgenstein was not much stronger than the two, but of this fact they could not be certain; and if they had not yet to consider themselves as entirely cut off, yet their further retreat became a subject of great anxiety. These circumstances had of necessity their weight with General York. General d'Auvray's letter, therefore, contained an instruction to communicate them to that officer, with the explanation, that if he should remain inattentive to them, and decline to put an end to his indecision, he would be treated like any other hostile commander, and all question of friendly agreement on any conditions would henceforth cease.

The second paper was the following letter of Marshal Macdonald to the Duke of Bassano, which had been intercepted by Wittgenstein.

This letter, dated Stalgen, 10th December, 1812, ran thus:—

 " My dear Duke,

  " You give me no news of yourself. I send to seek for some. An officer who is come in from Wilna brings some absurd reports from that town; he, however, assures us that he saw his Majesty the Emperor pass on his way to Kowno, whither your Excellency is to follow him.

 " I cannot believe all I have just been reading in the Russian bulletins, which I forward; although they quote names of persons, who, as I know, really belonged to the 2d and 9th corps. I expect from one moment to another to be enlightened by you. The shell has burst at last with General York; I have thought, that under such circumstances as are accredited, without being repudiated by the gentlemen of the Prussian staff, it was my duty to show more firmness. The body is sound, but they are spoiling it; the spirit is prodigiously changed; but a few favours, some rewards, and I shall easily set it up again, provided always, that the officers I designate are promptly removed: they will not be regretted, two thirds of the army detest them.

" In the name of Heaven, my dear Duke, write me
a word, that I may know what positions are about
to be taken up; I am concentrating myself more.

" MACDONALD."

The former of these two letters would not have
had weight with a man like York, but for a military
justification: if the Prussian court should require
one as against the French, it was important.

The second letter was calculated at the least to
call up in General York's mind all the feelings of
bitterness, which perhaps for some days past had
been diminished by the consciousness of his own
behaviour towards the writer.

As the Author entered General York's chamber,
the latter called out to him, " Keep off from me; I
will have nothing more to do with you: your
d——d Cossacks have let a letter of Macdonald's
pass through them, which brings me an order to
march on Piktupöhnen, in order there to effect our
junction. All doubt is now at an end; your troops
do not come up; you are too weak; march I must,
and I must excuse myself from all further negotiations, which may cost me my head." The Author
said that he would make no opposition to all this,
but begged for a candle, as he had letters to show
the General; and, as the latter seemed still to hesitate, the Author added, " Your Excellency will
not surely place me in the embarrassment of de-
parting without having executed my commission."
The General ordered candles, and called in Colonel

Roeder, the chief of his staff, from the antechamber.
The letters were read. After a pause of an instant,
the General said, " Clausewitz, you are a Prussian;
do you believe that the letter of General D'Auvray
is sincere, and that Wittgenstein's troops will really
be at the points he mentions by the 31st? Can you
give me your word of honour to this?" The Author
replied, " I pledge myself for the sincerity of this
letter, upon the knowledge I have of General
D'Auvray and the other men of Wittgenstein's
head-quarters; whether the dispositions he an-
nounces can be accomplished as he lays down, I
certainly cannot pledge myself; for your Excellency
knows that in war we must often fall short of the
line we have drawn for ourselves." The General
was silent for a few minutes of earnest reflection,
then held out his hand to the Author, and said,
" You have me. Tell General Diebitsch that we
must confer early to-morrow at the mill of Pos-
cherun, and that I am now firmly determined to
separate myself from the French and their cause."
The hour was fixed for 8 A. M. After this was settled, the General added, " But I will not do the
thing by halves, I will get you Massenbach also." He
called in an officer who was of Massenbach's cavalry,
and who had just left them. Much like Schiller's
Wallenstein, he asked, walking up and down the
room the while, " What say your regiments?" The
officer broke out with enthusiasm at the idea of a
riddance from the French alliance, and said, that
every man of the troops in question felt the same.

" You young ones may talk; but my older head is shaking on my shoulders," replied the General.

The Author returned, thoroughly satisfied, to Willkischken, and on the following morning accompanied General Diebitsch to the mill, where they found General York, attended by the Colonel von Roeder, and his first aide-de-camp, the Major von Seydlitz. Besides the Author, the Count Dohna alone accompanied General Diebitsch, so that the negotiation was confined to pure Prussians.

The convention is widely extant in print. We content ourselves here with saying, that, by its articles, the Prussian corps is declared neutral, and a district assigned to it as neutral ground in Prussian Lithuania on the Russian frontier. Should the convention be rejected by either of the sovereigns, the Prussians obtained a free march home in the shortest direction; but engaged themselves, should the rejection take place on the part of the King of Prussia, not to serve against the Russians for the space of two months.

General York had despatched, on the 26th, Major the Count von Henkel, one of the King's aide-de-camps, who happened to be with the army, to Berlin, to give the King preliminary knowledge of proceedings. He now sent off Major von Thile of his staff with the convention.

General York wrote at the end of the letter he sent with this, — "I willingly lay my head at your Majesty's feet if I have done wrong. I would die with joy and resignation at least to avoid the having failed in my duty as a true Prussian and faithful subject. Now or never is the moment when your Majesty may tear yourself from the extravagant demands of an ally, whose intentions towards Prussia, in the event of his success, were involved in a mystery which justified anxiety. This is the view by which I have been guided. Heaven grant that it may lead to the welfare of our country!"

General von Massenbach was with six battalions and one squadron in Tilsit, two other squadrons were in cantonments on the road to Insterburg, and seven were with the brigade of Bachelu in the neighbourhood of Ragnit. General York sent on the 30th an officer to Tilsit, and acquainted General Massenbach with the step which he had taken, and at the same time, to relieve him from responsibility, forwarded a positive order for his return from Tilsit to the main body. He transmitted by him the document in which he acquainted Marshal Macdonald with the step he had taken.

General Massenbach did not hesitate a moment in obeying the order to return. The circumstances at first appeared peculiarly favourable to its execution, as in Tilsit there was nothing but his own six battalions, and the troops of the division Grandjean were in distant quarters. In the night, however, of the 30th, as he was about to execute the order, several regiments of the division Heudelet came in accidentally from Königsberg, and others, as also the division Grandjean, were expected.

General Massenbach believed that these arrivals might be directed against himself, and thought it better, under the circumstances, not to break up his quarters in the night, but to wait for day, under the idea that by that time the suspicions might be allayed. This reasoning would appear erroneous: if the French already entertained suspicion, they would surely retain it by day. It is, however, certainly true that it is easier by day to adopt suitable measures, and all that was to be feared was, that by that time suspicion might amount to certainty. This did not prove to be the case; the troops had not been collected in the view of employing them against Massenbach; and the latter was able, at 8 A. M. on the 31st, quietly to cross the Memel river, and march to meet the Russians.

General Macdonald, finally acquainted with the occurrence by the letters which Generals York and Massenbach had prepared and forwarded to him after it was completed, behaved himself very nobly. He released the Lieutenant von Korf, who commanded a detachment of thirty horse at his headquarters, and who could not be carried off with the rest, with friendly expressions, and presents to officers and men.

By the Prussian troops the convention was accepted with enthusiastic acclamation.

What induced General York to delay his decision

so long appears in part from our narrative. Want of decision of character had least of all to do with it. He hoped that his position would deteriorate in a military view; that other Russian divisions would come up and give better pretexts for his conduct. He attained this object; for, on the one hand, General Lewis had so far approached as to be in communication with Diebitsch; on the other, the divisions of the Wittgenstein army, which had headed Macdonald, might be played off with effect in the event of a legal defence of General York being called for. General York was also anxious to wait the arrival of his aide-de-camp, Major von Seydlitz, from Berlin, which was to be expected at any instant. He gained this object also, for this officer reached Tauroggen early on the 29th. The purport of his instructions as to the political part of his mission was never known. It is probable that at Berlin he had found that this was not held to be the moment for a rupture of the alliance with France, and that previous concert with Austria was there considered necessary. The answer then was probably negative, that is, silence. Had it been conceived in Berlin that General York could take so bold a step as he did, they would probably have issued a direct declaration against it, and in that case the General would not have ventured. This, however, was fortunately not the case; and as Major von Seydlitz, in whom the General placed great confidence, and on whose personal statements much depended, himself was strongly under the conviction that it was both in the power and the duty of Prussia to throw off the French yoke at this moment, he had seen things at Berlin in the light of this preconceived opinion, and had so far co-operated there with General York. York saw plainly that he was incurring still great hazard, but his hands at least were not absolutely tied.

On the other hand, judging of men and things as they are, we must say that such a determination as that adopted by York requires its time to ripen, and that if this process is to be called indecision, the last despatches brought to him by the Author were well calculated to overcome it. As every day had aggravated his culpability, it required at last but a slight assault to remove from him all thought of returning on his path.

The conduct of General Diebitsch throughout the transaction was most praiseworthy; in evincing towards General York as much confidence as his own responsibility allowed him, in displaying throughout an unprejudiced, frank, and noble bearing, and appearing to feel only for the common interest, and as much for Prussia as for Russia, in rejecting all appearance of superiority in arms, all pride of victory, and all appearance of either Russian vanity or rudeness, he facilitated to General York the execution of a task very difficult in itself, and which under conditions less favourable would probably not have been brought to maturity.

The Author looks back with satisfaction to a little

scene which occurred in Willkischken. In the night of the 28th, as the Author had just returned from General York, General Diebitsch entered the room much discomposed, and told the Author that he had just received intelligence that a patrole of Cossacks, which had been despatched to carry a letter for General D'Auvray to Ragnit had been captured by the enemy. This letter, or rather scrap, contained an account, written, moreover, in French, briefly detailing how far progress had been made with General York, by which, should it fall into French hands, General York must be to the last degree compromised. General Diebitsch was beside himself at the reflection of being chargeable with this misfortune to the Prussian. He urged the Author in supplicatory language to return immediately to General York, to make an honourable confession of what had occurred. The commission was not a pleasant one, but the Author willingly undertook it. The sledge was at the door when the officer (Uradnick) of the Cossacks entered, and informed General Diebitsch that he had been attacked, and his people dispersed. " And the letter?" cried the General in haste. " It is here," quietly replied the Cossack, holding it out to the General. The latter fell on the neck of the Author, and wept.

Immediately on hearing of the secession of the Prussians, Macdonald had marched from Tilsit to Mehlaucken, which lies at the entrance of the forest. He met on this road with neither Wittgen-

stein nor Scheppelow, but only with some Cossack
regiments which belonged to the division of General
Kutusow.   They of course retired out of his way,
and he reached Mehlaucken safely, but hotly
pursued by Diebitsch and Kutusow.

General Scheppelow had, by a mistake of the
name, marched on the 31st to Szillen, instead of
Schillupischken, situated on the road from Tilsit to
Insterburg.   As Macdonald did not take this road,
he was perfectly useless.   General Wittgenstein
was much incensed, and deprived him of the command of the advanced guard.   Wittgenstein himself, however, as he had reached Löbegallen on the
29th, which is only some five miles from Schillupischken, might have easily gained this point by
the 31st in good time.   He came, however, only as
far as Sommeran: the badness of the roads, the exhaustion of the troops, the necessity of extension
for quarters, may be his excuse for making no
forced marches; but the main reason was, that the
energy began to flag, and that after such enormous
results men began to think that no more exertion
was required, and it was better to spare their own
people.

Wittgenstein nevertheless followed close on Macdonald's track to Königsberg, prevented him from
collecting his strength in that place, and rendered
impossible the idea of a defence of East Prussia by
the French.   Thus the question so often debated
at the Russian head-quarters, whether the frontier
should be crossed or not, was practically decided;

for after Wittgenstein had once reached Königsberg it was necessary that he should be supported, and Tschitschagow received orders to follow him by Gumbinnen. Both then followed the route of the French to the Vistula.

At this time Tschitschagow, as the older general, had the chief command of the troops which had crossed the Prussian frontier. Wittgenstein was so offended at this, that under pretence of illness he remained at Königsberg. The affair, however, was soon arranged. Tschitschagow remained before Thorn, and Wittgenstein, after leaving 10,000 men before Dantzick, crossed the Vistula with the remainder at Konitz, where he halted some weeks, and then marched upon Berlin, which he entered in the beginning of March.

If Wittgenstein, as we may well suppose, did not pursue this course without orders from Kutusow and the Emperor, he yet gave the first impulse to this continuation of the offensive as far as the Elbe, and drew the mass along with him. Although General York had had the address to prepare the King by two successive messages for such a step as he contemplated, yet was the King most disagreeably surprised by the convention. He found himself placed in serious embarrassment by the independent action of his general. The time seemed to him not yet arrived for an alteration of his political relations; and supposing it to be arrived, it seemed to him neither necessary nor becoming that a general officer should take upon himself the decision. This

reasoning was natural at Berlin, for there the full
extent of the destruction of the French army was
not yet perceived. As little were the consequences
embraced of General York's secession from the line
of combatants in their effect on the whole war.
His treaty then was necessarily looked upon as
an unprofitable act of independent assumption of
authority.

The calmer consideration, however, of the circumstances, a consultation with Baron Hardenberg,
might, perhaps, have already given rise to the idea
in the king's mind that it was neither the duty nor
the interest of Prussia to adhere to France in the
storm of calamity which she had brought upon
herself.

It was, therefore, determined at this difficult
crisis to avoid as far as possible any distinct declaration, and to steer as cautiously as might be.

The measure was to be disapproved, for form's
sake; the treaty not confirmed; the command of
the corps made over to General Kleist; an inquiry
suspended over General York; another contingent
promised; and the Prince Hatzfeld sent to Paris
with all these assurances. These were all proceedings which could have no great influence in the
scale of political affairs; but with these the French
were for the present forced to content themselves.

An aide-de-camp of the King, Lieutenant-Colonel
von Natzmer, was sent to General York with these
announcements. It so happened, however, that

the corps of York was in the rear of Wittgenstein, and that it was thus necessary for Lieutenant-Colonel Natzmer to pass through the Russians. He could not do this secretly, nor had he orders to attempt it; but he went to Wittgenstein and asked his permission for the transit. Wittgenstein asked him what were his instructions? He replied, that he had orders to effect the removal of General York from his command, and to transfer it to General Kleist. " In this case," said Wittgenstein, " you will not pass my posts. Have you any further commission?" The Lieutenant-colonel admitted that he was charged with a letter for the Emperor of Russia. " Ah, then, with the greatest satisfaction I shall give you leave for its delivery." A light sledge was produced; a Russian officer put himself into it with the Lieutenant-colonel, and they started for Wilna. This took place in the middle of January. General York remained in possession of his doubtful functions. In Berlin they became daily better acquainted with the annihilation of the French. The idea of the possibility of resistance gained ground from hour to hour, and within a month of the departure of Lieutenant-colonel Natzmer no doubt remained as to the course which Prussia ought to adopt. The King left Potsdam for Breslau. Wittgenstein entered Berlin the 7th of March. York marched behind him, and entered on the 17th. A document was issued from Breslau of the same date, declaring, that after an inquiry General York had been found free from blame, and was therefore restored to his command; and of the same date was the proclamation to the Prussian army and people.

This cursory view of the consequences of the Russian Campaign, of the running off of the mass of waters which had been collected, has been necessary, to place in a clear light the importance of the York convention.

Had York re-united himself with Macdonald, the latter, strengthened by the division of Heudelet which was coming up from Königsberg, would have formed a mass of 30,000 men behind the Niemen. As the main army had halted in Wilna, and Tschitschagow had received orders not to cross the frontier, and Wittgenstein was not more than 25,000 strong, including the troops arrived from Riga, it is not conceivable that Wittgenstein on his own responsibility would have ventured to cross the Niemen, there to offer battle to Macdonald, and carry the war into the heart of Prussia. It stands indeed, in Buturlin's History of the Campaign, that Wittgenstein had been at first directed to move from the neighbourhood of Wilna on Gumbinnen, but had been compelled by the badness of the roads near the Niemen to take a more northerly direction. We can, however, ascribe but little authority to this unintelligible or rather unintelligent portion of his work. The direction of Gumbinnen and that of Wilkomir are too wide of one another to allow us to attribute the same view to the two. The Russians at Wilna hardly contemplated the pushing forward a body of 25,000 men far into Prussia. According to the Author's recollection of what passed at the head-quarters of Wittgenstein, that general urged and carried the point of the successive advance towards Königsberg for the purpose of cutting off Macdonald, and then the pursuit of that Marshal to the Vistula. Wittgenstein, however, by Macdonald's delay, by the separation of Macdonald from York, by the negotiations, and, finally, by the conclusion of the convention, and the danger which Macdonald incurred, was drawn onward from one step to another, and things would have been far otherwise, if 30,000 men had been in waiting for the Russians behind the Niemen, or even behind the Pregel. It is next to certain that the Russian Campaign would have found its limit on the Prussian frontier.

Although we are not inclined to attribute the phenomena of this world each to an individual cause, but rather to consider them ever as results of many co-operating forces, so that the failure of a single member never produces a total alteration of the entire frame, we must still admit, that great results have often arisen from apparently trifling causes; and that a cause standing by itself, and therefore the more exposed to chances, has had very universal effects.

Thus it is with the York convention. It were unreasonable to suppose that, but for the resolution adopted by General York at Tauroggen, Buonaparte would still have been on the throne, and the

French masters of Europe; for the great result to
the contrary flowed from an endless variety of
causes, or rather forces, most of which were independent of General York: it is not, however, to be
denied, that his resolution had enormous consequences, and probably materially accelerated the
result.

It may now be allowed the Author to give his
opinion on Buonaparte's plan of operation in this
much-discussed campaign.

Buonaparte determined to conduct and terminate
the war in Russia as he had so many others. To
begin with decisive battles, and to profit by their
advantages; to gain others still more decisive, and
thus to go on playing double or quits till he broke
the bank—this was his manner; and we must
admit, that to this manner he owed the enormous
success of his career; and that the attainment of
such success was scarcely conceivable in any other
manner.

In Spain it had failed. The Austrian campaign
of 1809 had saved Spain, by hindering him from
driving the English out of Portugal. He had since
subsided there into a defensive war, which cost him
prodigious exertions, and, to a certain extent, lamed
him of one arm. It is extraordinary, and perhaps
the greatest error he ever committed, that he did
not visit the Peninsula in person in 1810, in order
to end the war in Portugal, by which that in Spain
would by degrees have been extinguished; for the
Spanish insurrection and the Anglo-Portuguese

struggle incontestably fomented each other. Buonaparte would, however, have been always compelled
to leave a considerable army in Spain.

It was naturally, and also very justly, a main
object with him, in the case of this new war, to
avoid being involved in a similarly tedious and
costly defensive struggle, upon a theatre so much
more distant. He was then under a pressing necessity of ending the war in, at the most, two campaigns.

To beat the enemy—to shatter him—to gain the
capital—to drive the government into the last
corner of the empire—and then, while the confusion
was fresh, to dictate a peace—had been hitherto
the plan of operation in his wars. In the case of
Russia, he had against him the prodigious extent of
the empire, and the circumstance of its having two
capitals at a great distance from each other. He
hoped to balance the moral disadvantages of these
two circumstances by two others—by the weakness of the Russian government, and the dissension
which he might hope to succeed in establishing between that government and the *noblesse*. He was
deceived in both these grounds of reliance; and this
it was which made the desertion and destruction of
Moscow so vexatious to him. He had hoped, from
that centre, to influence by opinion Petersburgh
and the whole of Russia.

That under these circumstances Buonaparte
should attempt to reach Moscow at a rush was only
natural.

The effect of territorial extension, and of a possible national war—in short, the pressure of a vast
state with its whole weight—could only make itself
felt after a season, and might be overwhelming, if
not itself overwhelmed, at the first onset.

If Buonaparte was really obliged to calculate on
ending the war in two campaigns, it then made a
great difference, whether he conquered Moscow or
not in the first.   This capital once taken, he might
hope to undermine the preparations for further resistance, by imposing with the force which he had
remaining—to mislead public opinion—to set feeling at variance with duty.

If Moscow remained in the hands of the
Russians, perhaps a resistance for the next campaign might form itself on that basis to which the
necessarily weakened force of Buonaparte would be
unequal.   In short, with the conquest of Moscow,
he thought himself over the ridge.

This has always appeared to us the natural
view for a man like Buonaparte.   The question
arises, whether this plan was altogether impracticable, and whether there was not another to be
preferred to it?

We are not of such opinion.   The Russian army
might be beaten, scattered: Moscow might be conquered in one campaign; but we are of opinion
that one essential condition was wanting in Buonaparte's execution of the plan—this was to remain
formidable after the acquisition of Moscow.

We believe that this was neglected by Buonaparte only in consequence of his characteristic negligence in such matters.

He reached Moscow with 90,000 men, he should have reached it with 200,000.

This would have been possible if he had handled his army with more care and forbearance. But these were qualities unknown to him. He would, perhaps, have lost 30,000 men fewer in action if he had not chosen on every occasion to take the bull by the horns. With more precaution and better regulations as to subsistence, with more careful consideration of the direction of his marches, which would have prevented the unnecessary and enormous accumulation of masses on one and the same road, he would have obviated the starvation which attended his advance from its outset, and have preserved his army in a more effective condition.

Whether 200,000 men placed in the heart of the Russian empire would have produced the requisite moral effect, and commanded a peace, is certainly still a question; but it seems to us that it was allowable to reason *à priori* to that effect. It was not to be anticipated with certainty that the Russians would desert and destroy the city, and enter upon a war of extermination; perhaps it was not probable: if they were to do so, however, the whole object of the war was frustrated, carry it on as he would.

It is, moreover, to be considered as a great neglect on the part of Buonaparte to have made so little preparation as he did for retreat.

If Wilna, Minsk, Polozk, Witebsk, and Smolensko, had been strengthened with works and
sufficient pallisades, and each garrisoned with from
5000 to 6000 men, the retreat would have been facilitated in more than one respect, especially in the
matter of subsistence.   It is sufficient to mention
here the convoy of 700 oxen carried off by the
Cossacks in the neighbourhood of Smolensko.   If
we consider that the army would also have both
reached and quitted Moscow in greater force, we
may conceive that the retreat would have lost its
character of utter destruction.

What, then, was the other plan which has been
put forward after the event, as the more judicious,
or, as its advocates term it, the more methodical?

According to this, Buonaparte should have
halted on the Dnieper and Dwina, should at furthest have concluded his campaign with the occupation of Smolensko, should then have established
himself in the territory he had acquired, have
secured his flanks, acquiring thereby a better base,
have brought the Poles under arms, increasing
his offensive strength, and thus for the next campaign have secured the advantage of a better start,
and arrived in better wind at Moscow.

This sounds well, if not closely examined, and
especially if we omit to compare it with the views
entertained by Buonaparte in adopting the other
plan.

According to the plan suggested, Buonaparte
must have confined himself to the reduction of

Riga and Bobruisk, for these were the only two fortresses within the territory designated, and must have drawn for the winter a line of defence from the gulf of Riga, along the Dwina to Witebsk, thence to Smolensko, then along the Dnieper to somewhere near Rogatschef, then behind the Precipiez and Muchawetz rivers to the Bug, an extent of some 200 miles.

This implies a conclusion of the campaign without a victory over the Russian army, which was to remain to a certain extent intact, and Moscow not threatened. The Russian military, weak at the commencement, and certain to be nearly doubled in the progress of hostilities, would have had time to complete its strength, and then, in the course of the winter, to commence the offensive against the enormously extended line of the French. This was no part in Buonaparte's taste to play. Its worst feature was, that a victory in the field, if he could gain one, remained without positive effect; since, in the middle of winter, or even late in autumn, he could devise no further operation for his victorious troops, no object on which to direct them. He could then do nothing more than parry without thrusting in return.

Then the details of execution!—How was he to dispose his army? In quarters? That for corps of moderate strength was only possible in the vicinity of large towns. Encamp them? Impossible in winter. Had he, however, concentrated his forces in single towns, the intervening country was not his own, but belonged to the Cossacks.

The losses which the army would have suffered in the course of such a winter could not probably have been replaced by arming the Poles.

This armament, if investigated, presented great difficulties. First were excluded from it the Polish provinces in possession of Austria; next, those remaining in possession of Russia. On Austria's account, also, it could not be conducted in the sense in which the Poles could alone desire it; namely, the restoration of the old Polish kingdom. This lamed the enthusiasm. The main difficulty was, however, that a country which has been pressed upon by enormous military and foreign masses is not in a condition to make great military exertions. Extraordinary efforts on the part of the citizens of a state have their limits; if they are called for in one direction they cannot be available in another. If the peasant be compelled to remain on the road the entire day with his cattle, for the transport of the supplies of an army, if he has his house full of soldiers, if the proprietor must give up his stores for the said army's subsistence, when the first necessities are hourly pressing and barely provided for, voluntary offerings of money, money's worth, and personal service, are hardly to be looked for.

Concede we, nevertheless, the possibility that such a campaign might. have fulfilled its object, and prepared the way for a further advance in the following season. Let us, however, remember what we have to consider on the other side—that Buonaparte found the Russians but half prepared, that he could throw upon them an enormous superiority of force, with a fair prospect of forcing a victory, and giving to the execution of his undertaking the rapidity necessary for a surprise, with all but the certainty of gaining Moscow at one onset, with the possibility of having a peace in his pocket within a quarter of a year. Let us compare these views and reflections with the results of a so-called methodical campaign; it will be very doubtful, all things compared, whether Buonaparte's plan did not involve greater probability of final success than the other, and in this case it was, in fact, the methodical one, and the least audacious and hazardous of the two. However this may be, it is easy to understand that a man like Buonaparte did not hesitate between them.

The dangers of the moment are those by which men are chiefly influenced, and therefore that often appears a desperate course, which is in fact, in the last instance, the only road to safety, and the greatest evidence of foresight. It is seldom that mere acuteness of understanding suffices to fortify men to this degree, and the foresight which leads them in such paths can only be derived from an innate audacity of character. The famous conqueror in question was so far from deficient in this quality, that he would have chosen the most audacious course from inclination, even if his genius had not suggested it to him as the wisest.

We repeat it. He owed every thing to this boldness of determination, and his most brilliant campaigns would have been exposed to the same imputations as have attached to the one we have described, if they had not succeeded.

THE END.

Other titles of interest

**JOURNAL OF THE
WATERLOO CAMPAIGN**
General Cavalié Mercer
New afterword by
Philip J. Haythornthwaite
416 pp.
80651-7 $15.95

AMATEURS, TO ARMS!
A Military History of the War of 1812
John R. Elting
318 pp., 19 photos, 16 maps
80653-3 $14.95

THE ART OF WAR
Niccolò Machiavelli
Translated by Ellis Farneworth
Revised and with an introduction
by Neal Wood
336 pp. 80412-3 $12.95

**FIFTEEN DECISIVE
BATTLES OF THE WORLD**
From Marathon to Waterloo
Sir Edward S. Creasy
420 pp., 2 illus.
80559-6 $15.95

INVINCIBLE GENERALS
Philip J. Haythornthwaite
240 pp., 160 illus.,
29 maps and plans
80577-4 $16.95

**THE MILITARY MAXIMS
OF NAPOLEON**
Edited by William E. Cairnes
Introduction and commentary by
David G. Chandler
253 pp., 10 illus.
80618-5 $13.95

**THE GENERALSHIP OF
ALEXANDER THE GREAT**
J.F.C. Fuller
336 pp., 35 illus.,
80371-2 $14.95

GEORGE WASHINGTON
A Biography
Washington Irving
Edited and abridged with an
introduction by Charles Neider
790 pp., 3 illus, 5 maps
80593-6 $18.95

**GEORGE WASHINGTON'S
GENERALS AND OPPONENTS**
Their Exploits and Leadership
Edited by George Athan Billias
766 pp., 23 photos, 9 maps
80560-X $19.95

JULIUS CAESAR
Man, Soldier, and Tyrant
J.F.C. Fuller
336 pp., 17 illus.
80422-0 $13.95

SCIPIO AFRICANUS
Greater than Napoleon
B. H. Liddell Hart
New foreword by Michael Grant
304 pp., 3 illus., 7 maps
80583-9 $13.95

HANNIBAL
Theodore Ayrault Dodge
702 pp., 227 charts, maps, plans,
and illus.
80654-1 $19.95

THE WAR OF 1812
John K. Mahon
476 pp., 35 illus.
80429-8 $15.95

Available at your bookstore

OR ORDER DIRECTLY FROM

DA CAPO PRESS, INC.

1-800-321-0050